Ministero per i Beni e le Attività Culturali
Soprintendenza Speciale per il Polo Museale Veneziano

to my son Ezio

A better understanding and a fuller
evaluation of works in the Accademia
Galleries have been made possible
thanks in part to the excellent
restorations carried out by the personnel
of the Soprintendenza Speciale per
il Polo Museale Veneziano:
Rosa Bagarotto, Rossella Cavigli,
Luisa Gusmeroli, Chiara Maida,
Alfeo Michieletto, Luigi Sante Savio
and Gloria Tranquilli.
Other contributions have been made by:
Roberto Bergamaschi, Paola Borghese,
Lucia Castagna, Cooperativa C.B.C.,
Pierangela Formaggini and Giulio
Bono, Stella Foscarini Volpin,
Pierpaolo Monfardini, Ottorino
Nonfarmale, Sandra Pesso, Marica
Petkovic, Walter and Valentina Piovan,
Zelina Rado, Roberto Saccuman,
Ferruccio Volpin, Marco and Serafino
Volpin.
Sincere thanks are due to Roberto
Fontanari, Sandra Rossi, Maria Destà
for the precious collaboration.

Translation
Ivor Neil Coward
Aaron Curtis
Nicholas Holland

New Edition 2005
First Edition 1998

© Ministero per i Beni
e le Attività Culturali
Soprintendenza Speciale
per il Polo Museale Veneziano

An editorial realization by
Mondadori Electa S.p.A., Milan

www.electaweb.it

Ministero per i Beni e le Attività Culturali
Soprintendenza Speciale per il Polo Museale Veneziano

The Accademia Galleries in Venice

by
Giovanna Nepi Scirè

Electa

The Accademia Galleries

Introduction

In the early 1800s, the Galleries of the Accademia – containing the most important collection of 14th-18th century Venetian paintings – along with the Brera Picture Gallery and Bologna Accademia became a museum. Its political origins were closely connected to the local events that in those years had reduced Venice to little more than a prize passed around among the great European powers. With the annexation under the Napoleonic Kingdom of Italy after the treaty of Presburg signed on December 26, 1805, and through Napoleon's decrees in 1806, 1808 and 1810, all the public palazzi and religious buildings were closed, and some were even destroyed. The works of art that surfaced from these events and which were somehow not sold or lost, found protection in the new Galleries.

Originally, however, the Galleries' purpose was largely educational, as is shown in the decree of September 1, 1803, extended on February 12, 1807 also to Venice, which established that alongside an academy of fine arts divided into various faculties there would be a gallery for the "benefit of those who practise painting".

The Venetian Academy of Fine Arts was forced to relocate from the *Fonteghetto della Farina* (flour warehouse) to a group of buildings – also acquired following the Napoleonic suppressions – which included the convent of the Lateran Canons, designed by Andrea Palladio in 1561, the Chiesa della Carità, reconstructed by Bartolomeo Bon between 1441 and 1452, and the Scuola della Carità, maybe the first of the Venetian *Scuole Grandi*, founded in 1260. Thus there was also the problem of how to incorporate the works of art into structures whose original purpose was entirely different, and which were not connected to one another.

The Academy faced problems from the start, due to its relative distance from the city centre and its location on the other side of the Grand Canal. This situation was described in a painting by Canaletto now on display in the National Gallery of London, which shows, among other things, the campanile that has since collapsed. A further problem was the limited amount of space available for use without resorting to a vastly expensive remodelling project for the Palladio building. Nonetheless, the government's decision was unshakeable, and the Accademia – which had been considering the complex at Santi Giovanni e Paolo with its attached Scuola Grande di San Marco, or the Misericordia, or the church and monastery of Santa Caterina – found itself, instead, forcibly transferred to a location that was already recognised as completely inadequate.

The restructuring project was led by Giannantonio Selva and lasted until 1811. It was necessary to completely gut the church which, once the furnishings and altars were removed, was then divided horizontally and vertically to create five large rooms on the lower floor for the school and two on the upper floor to serve as exhibition rooms. These spaces were created

Canaletto, View of the Church of Santa Maria della Carità, *London, National Gallery*

9

Giuseppe Borsato,
Commemoration
of Canova in the Scuola
Grande della Carità,
Venice, Museo d'arte
moderna, Ca' Pesaro

after walling up the Gothic windows, with lighting coming from above. The buildings were connected by opening a passageway on the first floor at the back of the Sala dell'Albergo and constructing a short stairway which led through a foyer to the other rooms.

The Scuola della Carità underwent minor renovations, important work having been carried out already during the 18th century under the direction of Giorgio Massari and Bernardino Macaruzzi. In 1766 the ground floor entrance had been completely remodelled, while a few years earlier the façade had been renewed by opening the large doorway at the centre; this made the old stairs obsolete, and they were demolished. In their place, two twin fights of stairs leading up to the Chapter Hall (Room 1) were constructed based on models by Macaruzzi. The small façade remained which connected the church and school and which served as the entrance to the school itself with the once coloured statues depicting *Virgin and Child with Devoteres*, commissioned from him by the Guardian Grande Marco Zulian (1345), and *Saint Christopher* and *Saint Leonard* (1378). The 14th century doorway in the courtyard is still intact, although it has been walled in. It is topped by a coloured stone lunette with the symbol of the Carità, commemorating the plague of 1348.

The rooms of the Scuola della Carità were largely left unaltered: the wooden ceiling from the late 15th century is still in the Sala dell'Albergo (Room 24), as is the triptych by Antonio Vivarini and Giovanni d'Alemagna dated at 1446, and Titian's *Presentation* which dates from August 3l, 1534 to March 6, 1539. The other canvases in the cycle – the *Marriage of the Virgin* by Giampietro Silvio and the *Annunciation* by Girolamo

Dente, formerly in the Parish of Mason Vicentino, are now in the museum's storerooms.

Also intact – aside from the fact that the altar was removed – is the great Chapter Hall (Room 1), where the sumptuous ceiling remains on display with its deep blue and gold lacunars, carved by Marco Cozzi from 1461 to 1484. Originally there were five high reliefs depicting the *Madonna della Misericordia* and the symbols of the other *Scuole Grandi*. They were removed in 1814 and disappeared thereafter, replaced today by the *Holy Father* at the centre which has been attributed to Pier Maria Pennacchi and was originally in the Venetian oratory of San Girolamo, and by the four *Prophets* by Domenico Campagnola also attributed to Stefano dell'Arzere, from the Scuola della Madonna del Parto in Padua.

It proved decidedly more difficult to adapt the Palladian convent, however, especially since its integrity had already been somewhat compromised by a fire in 1630. To provide greater exhibition surface Selva approached it with caution: the arcades of the Ionic loggia were closed leaving some halfmoons for lighting; the windows on the Sant'Agnese canal were raised, and the cells on the top floor were modified to create the engraving school and lodgings for the professors.

Beginning on August 10, 1817, the gallery was opened to the public for a brief period, and had a great number of visitors. A painting made by Giuseppe Borsato in 1822 commemorating Canova portrays with almost photographic precision how the first room must have looked at the Accademia's opening – with not only the Veneto paintings of the 16th century, but also Titian's *Assumption* from the Frari, which had been secured in 1816 by the president Leopoldo Cicognara.

The first items to be included in the collection were: a small number of works being donations and trial works by the academicians which were brought over from the old Academy; some of the remaining paintings from the Scuola della Carità; Abbot Farsetti's collection of plasters, acquired from the Austrian government in 1805. Pietro Edwards was named the curator of the collection, had been in charge of public paintings from 1778 until the fall of the Republic. All the governments that followed in Venice found in him a highly competent and useful collaborator. He was employed by the French commissaries for the selection of the pieces to give to Napoleon in 1797, and performed a similar function under the Austrians and the Kingdom of Italy, at which time he received the title of "curator of state-owned holdings". However, the overlapping of responsibilities – at times contradictory – with the Accademia Galleries placed him in an ambiguous situation, and did not allow him to block the mass exodus of important pieces to Milan or the dispersion of many important works. Although the next secretary of the Accademia, Antonio Diedo, was responsible for choosing state-owned works destined for the Gallery itself, during the prolonged delivery period the more important works went to the Brera Gallery in Milan, while Titian's *Saint John the Baptist* was kept in Venice (in the church of Santa Maria Maggiore) only because of the mass outcry of the Venetian people. Luckily some paintings were added that France had returned, amongst which was Paolo Veronese's famous *Christ in the House of Levi*. Others were removed from Venetian churches, such as that of San Giobbe, and placed in the Accademia Galleries as a precautionary measure, and yet other paintings were added from the first private contributions to the Gallery.

Sezione sulla linea **C.D**

Sezione sulla linea **E.F.**

Important works were added to the Gallery by bequest: in 1816 Girolamo Molin provided many works including an interesting group by early painters that contained the *Stories of the Passion* from the Rimini school, triptychs by Alberegno and Jacobello del Fiore, the polyptych by Lorenzo Veneziano with the *Annunciation* and Giambono's *Paradise*. Canova's brother then donated the large plasters *Theseus* and *Hercules*, now on deposit at the Gipsoteca (Plaster Gallery) di Passagno. In 1833 (finalised in 1850) the bequest of Felicita Renier was added, with works such as *Saint Jerome* by Piero della Francesca, the *Madonna and Two Saints* and the *Madonna with Saints Catherine and Magdalene* by Giovanni Bellini, and Cima's *Deposition*. Lastly, in 1838 Girolamo Contarini donated his noteworthy collection of 188 paintings, which included Bellini's *Madonna degli Alberetti*, the *Madonna with Blessing Child* and the *Allegories*, Cima's *Madonna and Two Saints*, *The Wedding of Saint Catherine* by Boccaccio Boccaccino, the *Sacra Conversazione* attributed to Sebastiano del Piombo and six Venetian scenes by Pietro Longhi.

Some acquisitions – which were significant although relatively few considering the enormous availability on the market – further enriched the heritage. The collection nevertheless continued to favour and protect Venetian painting as it does now and so was not particularly suitable for a well-rounded artistic education. During the 1800s, much effort was made to balance out this situation until the end of the century, when interest in the educational aspect had all but vanished and with it the desire to expand the breadth of the Gallery's collection.

Nonetheless, in 1822 the Accademia anticipated the intentions of the Brera Gallery and, through Abbot Celotti, acquired Giuseppe Bossi's prestigious drawing collection, which boasted more than three thousand pieces and included – in addition to folios by Leonardo da Vinci among which the fa-

Sezione sulla linea G·H

F. Lazzari Dis. inc. A. Archi[...]
P.A. Veneta

mous *Vitruvian Man* – drawings from the Bolognese, Roman, Tuscan, Ligurian and Lombard schools, not to mention the German, French and Flemish schools that provided a certain uniformity to the collection of paintings. Two years later, again through Celotti, a body of 602 drawings from Giacomo Quarenghi was secured.

As the number of art works increased, the exhibition spaces became wholly insufficient and overcrowded. The plans for enlargement designed by Selva, who died in 1819, were carried out under the supervision of Francesco Lazzari, and provided for two large halls to the left of the Palladian convent (Rooms 10 and 11). In 1828 both these halls were built, and the first one was opened; the second was not completed until 1834. Between the two halls four Greek marble columns were transferred from the Scuola della Misericordia. In 1829 Lazzari completely remodelled the convent: in the courtyard he demolished the arches inspired by Palladian perspective and left intact by Selva, and expanded the ends with two intercolumniations. He reopened the walled up Ionic arches, which at a later time, along with the Doric arches, were fitted with large windows.

In 1830 the façade was also modified: the emblems of La Carità were replaced with those of the Accademia, windows were opened in the niches, and a sculpture – now in the Public Gardens – by Antonio Giacarelli of *Minerva Seated upon the Adriatic Lion* was placed at the top.

During this time, the large room on the ground floor was divided, giving the Galleries a separate entrance from that of the Scuola (shown also in Combatti's plan of 1847). It was also in this period that the painters and students of the Accademia decorated the lunettes on the ceiling of the first room with the portraits of the most important Veneto artists, replacing previous works that are now indecipherable. Lastly, between 1849 and 1856, all the rooms were connected together, with the construction of the *sale*

Francesco Lazzari, Section of the room used as a picture gallery and of the ground floor room, Venice, Correr Museum, Drawings and Prints Room

*Carlo Scarpa,
Project for the awning
for the* Madonna
*by Paolo Veneziano,
Room 1*

nuovissime (the "newest rooms", nowadays Rooms 6, 7, 8 and 9).

The collections were further expanded at this time, above all by the purchase from Emperor Franz Joseph in 1856 of several important paintings in the Manfrin Gallery, such as the *Madonna* by Nicolò di Pietro, *Saint George* by Mantegna, Memling's *Portrait of a Young Man*, Giovanni Agostino da Lodi's *Lavander* and *La Vecchia (The Old Woman)* by Giorgione.

Initially, the annexation to the Kingdom of Italy did not bring about large scale changes but, from 1870 onwards, the school gradually became separate from the Accademia Galleries. This took place through various stages, including decrees in 1878 and 1879. The collection, entrusted to the supervision of the president of the Accademia, was officially delivered to him on January 15, 1881, while on March 13, 1882, final independence was sanctioned for both the school and the Accademia Galleries.

In 1895 the director, Giulio Cantalamessa, oversaw a radical reorganization of the painting collection, including a new home for the *Assumption* (Room 2) based on a project by Giacomo Franco. By eliminating works by artists of the 1800s and consolidating the few paintings from other Italian and foreign schools, he tried for the first time to establish a chronological order. The unitary cycles from the 15th century schools of San Giovanni Evangelista and Sant'Orsola – formerly dispersed – were regrouped

Soprintendenza per i Beni Artistici e
Storici di Venezia

Vittore Carpaccio
Ritorno degli ambasciatori
Venezia, Gallerie dell'Accademia

I Musei Italiani

Electa | **LEM**

Published and distributed by **Electa-LEM** Milano. Printed in Italy. Riproduzione vietata

Codice CL2002

9 788883 522888

into the church. The *Stories of Saint Ursula* were housed in one of the new octagonal spaces, with lighting from above, that would not actually replicate their original space (also due to insufficient information in that regard), but rather would serve to enhance the continuity of the pictorial narrative. 16th century Veneto paintings were placed in the large halls. Reacting probably to public opinion, Cantalamessa returned Titian's *Presentation* to the Sala dell'Albergo, where it had been located until 1828, believing correctly that it was preferable to respect the vision of the artist regarding the positioning and scanty lighting of the painting. The 18th century stone benches were then replaced with the 16th century dossals seen today. He also removed the bronzes, which were later brought together again in the G. Franchetti Gallery at Ca' d'Oro. Cantalamessa thus established what has remained the primary focus of the Accademia: a collection of Veneto painting from the 14th to the 18th centuries. Cantalamessa also enriched the collection, adding *Saints Peter and Paul* by Crivelli, works by Cosmè Tura, Basaiti's *Saint George*, Palma il Vecchio's *Sacred Conversation*, the *Wedding of Saint Catherine* by Lorenzo Veneziano, Paolo Veronese's *Hercules and Ceres*, and two early works by Tiepolo.

Cantalamessa was succeeded by Gino Fogolari in 1905, and little was done to the Accademia itself, although the collection of drawings and paintings

Carlo Scarpa, Project for the "compan" in the entrance

Carlo Scarpa, Project for the support for Giambattista Piazzetta's The Fortune Teller

continued to expand under his long direction, with the acquisition of two more early works by Tiepolo, various pendants, the *Death of the Virgin* by Pennacchi, the organ doors by Bellini originally at the Miracoli, Romanino's *Pietà*, the *Crucifixion of Saint Peter* by Luca Giordano, Strozzi's *Supper*, the *Portrait* by Fra' Galgario, Paolo Veneziano's *Madonna*, Tiepolo's draft of *The Exaltation of the Cross*, and lastly in 1932 Giorgione's *Tempesta*. After World War I, Fogolari lobbied for important pieces of art which had originally belonged to Venice to be returned from Austria.

During the war, the most important paintings had been kept in Florence. From 1921 to 1923, as these pieces were being returned, the museum was again remodelled. The Accademia suffered the loss of Titian's *Assumption*, which was returned to the Church of the Frari; the room that had been de-

16

signed for the large canvas seemed and remains disproportionate. The two rooms dedicated to the canvases of the *Ursula* cycle and the *Cross* cycle were eliminated, creating one large space with apses and restoring the truss ceiling and the Gothic windows on the side walls. The canvases with the *Miracles of the Cross* remained there, while the *Stories of Saint Ursula* were displayed in the small room where they are still kept today (Room 21): a largely arbitrary reconstruction of the room with choir stalls and backs from other locations.

A more "original" arrangement was given to the rooms dedicated to the small 18th century works (Room 17), incorporating imitation materials and an antique door originally from Ca' Rezzonico, where it has returned on deposit. 18th century doors, probably removed from a palazzo in Brescia and painted by Pietro Scalvini and Saverio Gandini, were purchased in 1912 and installed in the Palladian loggia, where they are still seen today. As under the direction of Cantalamessa, once again the works from the 19th century were removed and placed in storage at Ca' Pesaro; a similar fate awaited the paintings from foreign schools, which were moved to the G. Franchetti Gallery in the Ca' d'Oro. The immediate need to implement more modern criteria for the museum reached its culmination during the 1940s, and especially after direction of the Accademia passed to Vittorio Moschini in 1941. Moschini worked with Carlo Scarpa even while World War II was underway to formulate a more articulate restructuring, including the construction of a large new building to add to the 19th century halls and to attempt a chronological arrangement. The urgency to rebuild other Italian museums made it impossible to carry out the vast transformations that they had planned, but nonetheless a renovation project was begun which marked the end of a museum model that had remained unchanged since the turn of the century.

Work was begun in 1945 and lasted until 1960, involving the drastic elimination of the older rooms, carpeting, wooden skirting boards, imitation frames; these materials were replaced with a more neutral plaster with a special grain, warm-toned woods, jute, fustian, iron and glass, all carefully chosen and meticulously arranged. Given the space limitations and the fixed position of some of the larger canvases, a more logical itinerary through the museum was sought out, with a more careful selection of the works on display. The following year, the *Miracles of the Cross* paintings were re-grouped in a special room built in 1949 (Room 20) next to the hallway leading to the *Ursula* Room, and the two rooms – which were to house the closely related cycles – were connected by a small platform. As a result of this first project, which was improved later in 1959 and 1960, the room assumed its present appearance. Also in 1947, the furnishing and arrangement of the *Ursula* Room was completed, eliminating the previous design – which was completely anachronistic – and also that of the 18th century rooms, combining them into one larger room.

The following year, extensive imitation parts of the original wall decoration were removed from the church, and four new skylights were added to provide light from above. The 15th century paintings were arranged on panels, almost giving the appearance of a temporary exhibition, out of respect for the original architectural structure. Between 1950 and 1952 the first room was reorganised: the windows which had been walled in during the 19th century to increase the display area were reopened, and some fragments of late 14th century frescos were revealed along the walls, while the view into the disproportionate room (originally for Titian's *Assumption*) was blocked with a wide brick panel where the *Lion* polyptych by Lorenzo Veneziano was to be placed. Between 1950 and 1953 the new entrance was created with its now famous compass, while in 1955 Rooms 4 and 5 were completed for the display of small sized masterpieces and Giorgione's *Tempesta*, finally removed from the isolated pre-war location. Under the direction of Francesco Valcanover from 1961 to 1977, special attention was given to the improvement of services, from the most basic ones to the installation of new fire prevention and anti-theft systems. Further efforts were dedicated to the preservation of drawings, collected on the top floor in air-conditioned rooms and special cases. The museum was equipped with more rational and efficient storage facilities, while in the church in the room opposite the apses a space was created dedicated to Gino Fogolari for temporary exhibitions and shows. The collection did not grow in the years immediately after the war. In 1949 Guido Cagnola generously donated a notebook of sketches by Canaletto depicting various Venetian scenes, an invaluable document for tracing the creative process in his paintings. Acquisitions were made again in the 1970s: in 1971 *Fire in the Oil Warehouse at San Marcuola* by Francesco Guardi was added, as was Bartolomeo Montagna's panel *Saint Peter and a Donor*; in 1979 Count Nani Mocenigo sold the large Longhi painting of *The Family of Procurator Luigi Pisani*; in 1981 the *Portrait of the Knight Giovanni Grimani* by Strozzi was obtained from Palazzo Barbaro Curtis through a

Accademia Galleries,
Room 9, visitor's facilities

Accademia Galleries, Church of the Carità view with the canvases of the Sala dell'Albergo of the Scuola di San Marco

purchase option; in 1983 Jacopo Bassano's *Adoration of the Shepherds* was acquired from the Giusti del Giardino family. In 1987 two *Putti with Scrolls* and two allegories of *Justice* and *Patience* were obtained, remnants of the ceiling made by Giorgio Vasari in 1542 for a room in Palazzo Corner on the Grand Canal. While over the course of 2002 a third putto with a plaque was recovered and the central part depicting *Charity* was obtained from the Pinacoteca di Brera, and negotiations commenced simultaneously for the acquisition of the two remaining panels with *Faith* and *Religion*, both in private collections in London. In 1983, after the death of Rodolfo Siviero – the former head of the office for the recovery works of art "exported" to Germany before and during World War II, and to other countries in later years – Francesco Valcanolver successfully and courageously recovered at least thirty works from those that had been returned from abroad, and which had remained in Palazzo Pitti in Florence for decades while delivery plans were stalled and delayed. Unfortunately the returned works were always fewer than those requested, but in 1988 seven paintings were obtained, including an episode from *Jerusalem Delivered* by Giannantonio Guardi, which was not previously in the Galleries, two small *Bacchanals* by Sebastiano Ricci, and two *capricci* attributed to Canaletto.

In 1989 *The Great Wood* by Anton Francesco Peruzzini and Alessandro Magnasco was acquired through a purchase option. In 1995 Giuseppe Angeli's *Solletico* was acquired, and in 1997 thirteen large drawings by G.B. Piazzetta were obtained. In 1988, after the exhibition on the restorations of Paolo Veronese's works, his ceiling pieces were displayed in Room 6. In 1994 a picture gallery was opened in the long corridor of the Palladian hall on the second floor, allowing for eighty masterpieces to be displayed which had originally been kept in the archives. In 1996 Room 11 was remodelled, and all the remaining pieces by Tiepolo from the destroyed ceiling of the Church of the Scalzi were placed there. Later, the Chiesa della Carità was completed, and the canvases which were previously in the Sala dell'Albergo of the Scuola di San Marco were displayed there. Fibre-optic lighting was installed in Rooms 4 and 5, and in the small gallery of 18th century paintings. In 1997, a sales point was set up in room 9, while two windows have been reopened in Room 6, offering a view of Palladio's façade; but in spite of this the Accademia Gallery is still anxiously awaiting the reorganization of areas currently occupied by the Academy of Fine Arts in order to finally realize the project of the Grandi Gallerie.

With regard to this introduction, see especially: S. Moschini Marconi, *Gallerie dell'Accademia di Venezia. Opere d'arte dei secoli XIV e XV*, Rome 1955; and: E. Bassi, *Il complesso palladiano della Carità*, Milan 1980 and G. Nepi Scirè, *I capolavori dell'arte veneziana. Le Gallerie dell'Accademia di Venezia*, Verona 1991.

For the history of the collection of drawings at the Accademia Galleries, see also: G. Nepi Scirè. *Storia della collezione dei disegni*, Milan 1982.

The "Primitives"

This was the room where the chapter met of the great Scuola di Santa Maria della Carità, one the six *Scuole Grandi* of Venice. These schools were powerful secular guilds for devotion and assistance to the poor. The ceiling, which was built between 1461 and 1484 by Marco Cozzi of Vicenza – at the time a member of the Scuola – is made up of square lacunars with leaf decorations on the side and heads of angels with eight wings, each with different facial characteristics. The blue background and the original colours of the figures have resurfaced from the gilt decoration made in the 1700s thanks to a long restoration project completed in 1992.

The paintings in the compartments, however, do not belong to the original decoration: at the centre is the *Holy Father*, probably the work of Pier Maria Pennacchi (1464-1514/1515), while at the corners are the four *Prophets* attributed to Domenico Campagnola (1500-1564) or Stefano dell'Arzere (records from 1540 to 1575).

Paolo Veneziano,
Polyptych, detail

The polychrome marble floor dates to the remodelling of the 1700s. The rooms underwent other modifications at the beginning of the 1800s, when the entire complex of buildings became the Accademia: the back altar was removed, the windows were walled over to increase exhibition space and the original paintings were replaced with works that were to form the new gallery (including Titian's *Assumption*, now in the Church of the Frari). The present day configuration of the room is the work of Carlo Scarpa, begun in 1950. Scarpa reopened the windows, restored the fragments of the late 14th century fresco along the walls and arranged the gold backed paintings on the wooden panels with the iron bases that still support them today. Over the course of 2004 all the works in the room have been subjected to special maintenance; Scarpa's panels have been restored.

1a   1b   1c

1. **Jacobello del Fiore**
(recorded in Venice
from 1400 to 1439)

Justice and the Archangels
Panel, 208 × 194 cm
(central panel), 208 × 133
cm (Saint Michael),
208 × 163 cm (Saint Gabriel)
Acquisition: 1884,
following the Napoleonic
suppressions (cat. 15)
Latest restoration: 1997

Painted probably in 1421
for the seat of the
Magistrato del Proprio at
the Doge's Palace, which
oversaw the civil and
penal court. In the central
panel between two lions –
symbols of divine wisdom
– is Justice, who holds a
sword in the right hand
and scales in the left.
The closest iconographic
source for Saint Michael,
who holds up the scale
while slaying the dragon,
is found in a mosaic in St.
Mark's baptistery.
On the Latin writings
between the scrolls, the
archangel Gabriel entreats
the Virgin to guide men in
the darkness of their
actions, while Michael, the
warrior angel and defender
of the Church – in his dual
role as judge of souls and
fighter against the dragon, a
symbol of Satan – asks her
to levy rewards or
punishments according to
merit.
The wording behind

Justice "*I will carry out the
wishes of the angels and the
holy words, be mild towards
the pious, enemy of the evil
and disdainful of the proud*"
Is generally attributed in
Nordic art to Christ the
Judge.
Justice is clearly identified
with Venice, as it is also
featured on the relief of
the same period on the
west façade of the Doge's

Palace. The Venice–Justice
association, and that of
Peace is here enriched by
the Virgin Mary, since
peace and justice were
fundamental ideological
concepts of the Venetian
State.
This triptych was an
important official
commission for Jacobello.
Its complex symbolism
fully renders the spirit of

the Gothic with a
decorative aspect that
seems best defined as
"floral", as with
architecture and sculpture
of the time.
The piece was to be an
especially important
example for Michele
Giambono and Michele
di Matteo.

Paolo Veneziano

(active from 1333 to 1358
died before 1362)

2. *Polyptych*

Panels, gold background,
98 × 63 cm (central),
40 × 94 cm each (four
side panels), 26 x 19 cm
(above, six larger panels),
23 × 7 cm (above, four
smaller panels), 30 × 16
cm (the two top panels)
Acquisition: 1812,
following the Napoleonic
suppressions. The central
panel, which was taken to
Brera by mistake in 1808,
was united with the
complex only in 1950,
(cat. 21)
Latest restoration: 1951

At the centre, the
Coronation of the Virgin.
At the sides, the stories of
Christ. On the upper
part, at left: the Pentecost,
Saint Matthew, the
Vestment of Saint Claire,
Saint John, Saint Francis
gives his clothes to his
father; at right, Saint
Francis receiving the
stigmata, Saint Mark, the

death of Saint Francis,
Saint Luke, Christ the
Judge. At the centre: the
two prophets Isaiah and
Daniel.
The piece comes from
the Church of Santa
Chiara, as is attested by
the Franciscan images in
the upper part, and
especially – in the *Death
of Saint Francis* episode –
the small monk, probably
the commissioner of the
work.
Dating to around 1350,
the polyptych documents
the insertion of mainland
motifs into the Byzantine
influenced culture of
Venice, also revealed in
the *Coronation of the Virgin*
of 1324 in the National
Gallery of Washington.
These motifs become
more complex here, with
decorative effects and
more accentuated
Byzantine traits; indeed,
the Byzantine influence
in Paolo's work has led
some to suggest that he
travelled to
Constantinople, where he
obtained the new
elements he would later
introduce in his
paintings.
The piece reveals great
diversity between the
small side episodes and
the larger central figures,
which are extraordinarily
refined arabesques.
This divergence does not,
however, allow us to
suggest that other hands
were involved in the
creation of the
composition, especially
given the consistently
high quality of the work.
The artist alternates the
courtly and precious
Byzantine language of
the central part, with its
fixed iconic nature that
well suits the depiction of
an event taking place
outside normal time and
space, with precise
references to the western
cultural affinity for the
narrative unfolding of
'stories'.

3

3. *Virgin with Child and two Commissioners*

Panel, gold background,
142 × 90 cm,
157 × 105 cm
with the original frame
Acquisition: 1913 by
purchase (cat. 786)
Last restoration: 1952

The piece was acquired
in 1913 from the
Salvadori antiquary of
Venice. While the
original two-tone
'toothed' frame and the
old crossed support on
the back are still intact,
the work has lost the
veiling of the flesh-tones,
the lower inscription and
some of the colours in
the dress of the Virgin. It
was first recognised as a
work of Paolo Veneziano
in the catalogue of 1928,
and today it is
unquestionably accepted
as such.
Its similarity to the 1321
paliotto at Dignano,
which the painting
slightly postdates, points

to its having been
produced in the second
half of the 1330s.
The Virgin with the
infant Jesus in the clypeus
constitutes a Syrian
iconographic variant of
the *Playtera*, while the
gesture of sheltering the
two small devotees,
whose physical details
make them veritable
portraits, is an unusual
reminder of the *Madonna
della Misericordia*.
The monumentality of
the image of the Virgin –
"dark-faced like a Coptic
or Cretan inspired icon"
– and the harmonious
assimilation of eastern
and western elements,
together with the
humanity of the
commissioners, make this
arguably the artist's
masterpiece.

1

4

of the artist's masterpieces for the transparency of its colours and the elegance of its figures. It was completed after 1427, when there was still a wooden crucifix on the altar. It is likely that the commissioner of the piece was the convent prior, Fra' Bernardo de' Scapi, who, like the artist, was also from Bologna.

5. Lorenzo Veneziano
(records from 1356 to 1372)

Saint Peter, Saint Mark

Panel, gold background, 115 × 42 cm, 115 × 64 cm
Acquisition: 1812, following the Napoleonic suppressions, (cat. 5, 5a)
Latest restoration: 1948

Signed and dated 1371, these are the side panels of a disassembled polyptych. The centre panel (the *Resurrection*) is kept a the City Museum of Milan. The association of the founder of the Church with the protector of the Venetian state and the fact that the work comes from the Silk Office at Rialto reveal the diffusion of religious devotion in the public life of the city.

6. Giovanni da Bologna
(records from 1377 to 1389)

Madonna dell'Umiltà, Saints and Members of the Scuola di San Giovanni Evangelista

Panel, gold background, 111 × 99 cm
Acquisition: 1812, following the Napoleonic suppressions (cat. 17)
Latest restoration: 1948

A work from the early 1380s. Connections between the artistic culture of the Venetian lagoon and that of the Emilia region are evident here, for example in the naturalism of the flowery meadow. Below, the members hold up the standard of the Scuola di San Giovanni Evangelista, where the painting originated.

4. Michele di Matteo
(documented in Bologna from 1410 to 1469)

Polyptych

Panels; the polyptych is made up of two orders separated by an overlying border 21 × 225 cm, and an overlying predella 38 × 225 cm. Each order is composed of three panels: 111 × 64 cm (upper middle), 142 × 63 cm (lower middle), and 11 × 85 cm (upper side), 142 × 85 cm (lower side). Acquisition: 1812, following the Napoleonic suppressions, (cat. 24)
Latest restoration: 1979

On the lower order is depicted the *Virgin with Child and Four Angels*; to the left, *Saint Lucia and Saint Helena*; to the right *Mary Magdalene and Catherine of Alexandria*; on the pendentives are four panels with the *Doctors of the Church*. On the upper order at the centre is the *Crucifixion*; to the left the evangelists *Matthew and Mark*; to the right *John and Luke*. On the band separating the two orders in sixteen nooks are the *Redeemer* and Saints. On the predella are five stories about the discovery of the True Cross, from the left *Saint Helena arrives in Jerusalem, Saint Helena*

convenes the Jews who keep counsel, Judas refuses to reveal where the Cross is, but after falling in a well he shows its location and he himself digs to find it, Proof of the True Cross which revives a small boy, Adoration of the Cross while the devils flee. At Saint Catherine's feet is the signature: "Michael Mathei da Bononia F."
This comes from the Church of Sant'Elena, where it was situated on the altar of Saint Helena, erected in 1418 by Alessandro Borromei. The frame is from the original complex, but was restored in 1829.
The work is considered one

5a   6   5b

7. Veneto–Byzantine School – 14ᵗʰ Century

Virgin with Child

Panel, gold background, 77 × 38,5 cm
Acquisition: 1932, from the Duomo of Burano, (cat. 884)
Latest restoration: 1939

Panel originally in the Duomo of Burano. It is generally associated with the *Nursing Virgin* in the Marciano Museum but reveals a more accentuated Byzantine component.

8. Jacobello Alberegno (died before 1397)

Christ on the Cross, between the Virgin, Saint John, Saint Gregory and Saint Jerome.

Panel, gold background, 40,5 × 55 cm
Acquisition: 1816, bequest of Girolamo Molin (cat. 25)
Latest restoration: 1939

Dated to around the 1380s. The Virgin and Saint John are depicted at three quarter face, giving depth to the gold

background. The skull in the rocks at the foot of the cross is connected with an ancient Judeo-Christian cult for the burial of Abraham, a theme taken up often in 17ᵗʰ century sculpture and 14ᵗʰ and 15ᵗʰ century Tuscan painting.

1

7   8

9d   9c   9a   9b   9e

1

Lorenzo Veneziano
(records from 1356 to 1372)

9. *The Annunciation and Saint Gregory, Saint John the Baptist, Saint James and Saint Stephen*

Panels, gold backgrounds, 111 × 55 cm (central), 94 × 24 cm (sides)
Acquisition: 1812, following the Napoleonic suppressions, (cat. 9)
Latest restoration: 1988

On the step of the throne are the signature and the date of 1371. The original destination of the gold-backgrounded work is unknown. The use of the flowery meadow constitutes a new theme that would be widely developed by the International Gothic, and used previously by this artist in the panels in the Berlin Museum.

10. *Marriage of Saint Catherine*

Panel, gold background, 93 × 58 cm
Acquisition: 1900, donated by the Udine Seminary, (cat. 650)
Latest restoration: 1948

The artist's signature and the date of 2 February 1359 are visible below (according to the Veneto dating system, and therefore really 1360). The original location of the piece is unknown, but it is believed to have been the central part of a polyptych. Once owned by the Marin family in Venice, then it was acquired by Jacopo Danieli, passing on to Count Pellegrino of Zara, then to the Cernazai collection and finally to the Udine Seminary.

10

11. **Catarino**
(documented in Venice from 1362 to 1382)

Coronation of the Virgin

Panel, gold background, 89 × 60,5 cm
Acquisition: 1877, purchased from count Vincenzo Galli, (cat. 16)
Latest restoration: 1998

The work dates to 1375 and depicts Jesus and the Virgin seated on a single throne, placed against a background of the blue vault of heaven. In spite of the use of the same gestures and of rich colours the work appears less refined than Paolo Veneziano's treatment of the same subject.

12. **Michele Giambono**
(records from 1420 to 1462)

Saint James and Saints

Panel, gold background, 108 × 45 cm (central), 88 × 29 cm (sides)
Acquisition: 1812, following the Napoleonic suppressions (cat. 3)
Latest restoration: 1979

On the central part at the bottom is written: "Michael / Giambono Pinxit". Acquired in 1948 from the Scuola del Cristo on the Giudecca island, but it originally belonged to the Chiesa di San Giacomo on the Giudecca. The saint appears in the central part and is represented by the staff and the book opened to a part of the epistles written to the apostle (I, 22), while to his right stands Filippo Benizi, the founder of the Serviti, with no halo because he was only canonised in 1671. Benizi appears holding the book of Psalms, opened to the verse "Servus Tuus sum ego".
As a late work from around 1450, it suggests an awareness, if not an understanding, of the Tuscan artists working in Venice, especially Andrea del Castagno, with his frescos in the chapel of San Tarasio at San Zaccaria. At the Albertina in Vienna there is a drawing with variations of Venerable Phillip and Saint Michael.

11

12

13

13. Jacobello del Fiore
(records from 1400, died in 1439)

Madonna della Misericordia with Saints John the Baptist and John the Evangelist

Panel, gold background, 87 × 114 cm

14

Acquisition: 1816, a bequest of Girolamo Molin, (cat. 13)
Latest restoration: 1987

Its original location is unknown. At the centre are the date and signature: "1436 Jachomello de Flor pense", which may also have been written on the frame, now lost. The date is clearly incorrect, however, as it does not correspond with the stylistic nature of the piece. Although the iconographical motif of the *Platytera Madonna* and the *Madonna della Misericordia* together was taken from Paolo Veneziano, the painting appears to owe more to the influence of Gentile da Fabiano and Michelino da Besozzo. It is a variation of a subject treated earlier, in 1407, on the Montegranaro triptych (today in a private collection in Switzerland). Comparison with the Montegranaro triptych reveals a moore subtle elegance, less iconic fixedness and even some studied characterisation of the small worshipers kneeling in the meadow covered with small flowers. The work probably dates to between 1415 and 1420. In fact, it bears a similarity

with the *Leone Andante* in the Doge's Palace, signed and dated 1415, and was clearly painted before the sumptuous *Justice* triptych, which is from 1421. Considering these factors, 1416 would be a more correct hypothetical date for the completion of the piece. With the removal of the 18th century frame, some fragments were found that had not been altered by light or varnishes, and some test brush marks.

14. The 15th Century Venetian School

The Cross of Saint Theodore

Rock crystal and partially gilded silver, 92 × 43 cm, bronze base 46 cm high
Acquisition: 1919, passed, with the Napoleonic suppressions, into the collection of Count

Savorgnan, then to Abbat Luigi Celotti who sold it to the Emperor of Austria for the new Imperial Museum in Vienna. It was assigned to the Galleries with the post-war restitutions (s. 18)

Originally from the Scuola Grande di San Teodoro. Composed of rock crystal and partially decorated with silver, the piece is housed in a case designed by Carlo Scarpa made of glass, iron and an antique fragment of porphyry. This object echoes the influence of the Tuscan artists working in Venice whilst retaining gothic elements of Nordic extraction.

15. Venetian School of the Second Half of the 14th Century

Coronation of the Virgin and the Stories of Christ

Panel, gold background, 55 × 39 cm (central), 55 × 41 cm (sides)
Acquisition: 1816 (cat. 23)
Latest restoration: 1951-54

At the centre, the Coronation of the Virgin; at the sides, the Stories of Christ: the Nativity, Christ with the Doctors, the Last Supper, the Crucifixion, the Deposition, the Resurrection, the Ascension and the Pentecost. The paintings are part of a single group of unknown origin which had been separated and was reassembled in 1954.

16d

16c

16. **Jacobello Alberegno**

(died before 1397)

Polyptych of the Apocalypse

Panels, 95 × 61 cm (central), 45 × 32 cm, 45 × 33 cm, 44 × 33 cm, 45 × 32 cm
Acquisition: 1951, became State property after the Napoleonic suppressions. Five panels moved to the deposit of San Giovanni Evangelista from where, in 1838, the *Vision* and the *Judgement* were sent on to Vienna and then returned with the post-war restitutions of 1919. Displayed in the Museum on Torcello until 1948. In that year they were reunited with the others which, since 1840, had been in the Correr Museum. Finally, in 1951 the whole group was acquired and displayed by the Galleries of the Accademia (cat. 1000)
Latest restoration: 1952

The five panels depict one of the visions described by Saint John in the Apocalypse, with the steps marked by Roman numerals. The central panel shows Eternity in Glory, with the lamb between the four symbols of the evangelists (IV), with "six wings […] and full of eyes", adored by 24 elders; the side panels depict *The Harvest of the Earth* (XIV): "thrust in thy sickle, and reap: for the time is come for thee to reap; for the harvest of the earth is ripe" (14,5 - 16,1); Babylon (XVII), or "the great whore […] seated atop a beast […] with seven heads and ten horns" (16, 2 - 17, 8); the *Cavalcade of the Kings* (XIX): "And behold a white horse; horse and he who sat upon him […] on his head were many crowns; and the armies which were in heaven followed him upon white horses" (18, 18 - 19, 21) and the *Final Judgement* (XX): "I saw a great white throne and him that sat on it […] And I saw the dead, small and great, stand before God; and the books were opened […]" (20,11 - 22,5).

On the book that Christ holds open is written: "chi no / n è scri / ti.su / questo / libro // sera da / nadi".

Originally the work was housed in the Church of San Giovanni Evangelista on Torcello, which fell into ruin over the course of only a few decades until it was demolished.

The complex allegorical theme performs its didactic function with great clarity, while the figurative culture of Giusto de' Menabuoi is transposed in the more typically Venetian terms of chromatic sensibility and expressive strength. The Church of San Giovanni Evangelista on Torcello was reconstructed after a fire in 1343, providing us with a *post quem* date for the work sometime in the latter half of that century.

1

16a

16e

16b

17. Catarino
(documented in Venice
from 1362 to 1390)

*Coronation of the Virgin
and Angels*

Panel, golden background,
105 × 58 cm (central),
96 × 28 cm (sides)
Acquisition: 1902,
purchase of Tommaso
Mazzoli, (cat. 16)
Latest restoration: 1948

The original location of
the Triptych is unknown,
but it was probably
painted later than the
Coronation of the Virgin by
Paolo Veneziano of 1375
as is borne out by the
nonchalance of the
figures, the elegance of
Saint Lucia, inspired by
Lorenzo Veneziano, and
the rough features of
Saint Nicolas.

**18. Stefano "Plebanus"
di sant'Agnese**
(active from 1369 to
1385)

Coronation of the Virgin

Panel, golden background,
75 cm × 52 cm
Acquisition: 1816,
bequest of Girolamo
Molin, (cat. 21)
Latest restoration: 1951

The painting is signed
and dated 1381
("plebanus" means
parishioner). Although
the work is based on the
Coronation of the Virgin by
Paolo Veneziano, here it is
read with a full Gothic
sensitivity, evident in the
play of the perspective
planes and the use of
light and brilliant
colours.

19. **Antonio Vivarini**
(c. 1418/1420 – 1476/1484)

Virgin with Child

Panel, gold background,
64 × 41 cm
Acquisition: 1959, from
the parish of San Giorgio
delle Pertiche where it
had been deposited since
1846, (cat. 1236)
Latest restoration: 1958-59

The original location of
this devotional panel is
unknown. However, since
it came from state
holdings it must once
have been housed in a
public building, a theory
also supported by a 1711
inscription on the back
of the piece which refers
to a magistracy during
which time the work was
restored. The painting is
extremely contained, and
in spite of the retention
of the gold background it
reveals a knowledge of
new research on volume
and bright colours are
bright, techniques
proposed by the Tuscans,
and particularly
Masolino. It dates to
about 1440.

20. **Veneto School of
the End of the 14th
Century**

Portable Altar

Panel, gold background,
119 × 45 cm (central),
119 × 40 cm (sides)
Acquisition: 1812,
following the Napoleonic
suppressions, (cat. 14)
Latest restoration: 1950

On the central panel:
Madonna dell'Umiltà;
above: *Pietà*; at the sides:
the Saints James and
Francis, with the
instruments of the
Passion behind them. The
work dates to about
1385, and is from the
Chiesa di San Gregorio.

21. **Nicolò di Pietro**
(documented in Venice
from 1394 to 1427)

Saint Lawrence

Panel, gold background,
63 × 23 cm
Acquisition: 1816,
bequest of Girolamo
Molin, (cat. 20)
Latest restoration: 1951

Probably part of a lost
polyptych, the panel is
placed towards the later
phase of the artist's life.

19

20

1

21

que como sancta monika fi mandata
marito dai padre coin madre

23

22

22. **Nicolò di Pietro**
(documented in Venice
from 1394 to 1427)

Virgin with Child

Panel, gold background,
100 × 66 cm
Acquisition: 1856,
by purchase from the
Manfrini collection
(cat. 19)
Latest restoration: 1949

Under the footboard of
the throne is written:
"hoc / opus / fecit fiei /
dns vulcia / belgarcone /
civis.ya / driensis /
MCCCLXXXXIIII. Nichola
/ filus mri Petri pictoris
de vene / ciis pinxit hoc
opus qui mo / ratur in
chapite pontis paradixi",
which denotes the date
of 1394, the name of the
commissioner, the artist's
signature and his address
at the foot of the
Paradiso bridge.
The earliest well known
and dated work, the panel
is so cohesive and refined
that the question
regarding the artist's

previous training and
production has not yet
been fully answered, nor
has his role during the
transition from Venetian
painting of the 14th
century to that of the
15th been adequately
understood.
Compared with the
abstract nature of Paolo
Veneziano, the chromatic
elegance of Lorenzo, and
the decorativism of
Jacobello, Nicolò stands
out for his explorations
in the use of colour and
volume. As has often
been stated, Nicolò
looked significantly more
towards the artists of the
terra firma than to the
figurative artists, noting
such works as those of
Alitichiero and Avanzo,
the frescos in Treviso by
Tommaso da Modena,
and the works of Vitale
da Bologna and other
of his contemporaries
in Bologna.

23. **Antonio Vivarini**
(records from
c. 1418/20-1476/84)

Marriage of Saint Monica

Panel, 46 × 31 cm
Acquisition: 1816,
bequest of Girolamo
Molin (cat. 50)
Latest restoration: 1951

Dated to around 1441,
the panel was part of a
series of Stories placed
around a statue of Saint
Monica in the Church
of Santo Stefano. Below,
a caption explains the
depiction: "qui è como
sancta Monika fu
mandata a marito dal
padre e da la madre"
("here it is shown how
Saint Monica was sent to
marriage by her father
and mother"). Inspired by
the style of Masolino and
Paolo Uccello, the scene
reveals new elements
from the customs of the
time and a studied use
of perspective.

24. **Michele Giambono**
(records from
1420 to 1462)

*Coronation of the Virgin
in Heaven*

Panel, gold background,
228 × 177 cm with
gilded plaster decorations
Acquisition: 1816,
bequest of Girolamo
Molin (cat. 33)
Latest restoration: 1949

Probably painted for the
Church of Sant'Agnese
around the middle of the
15th century, the panel
repeats the same scheme
and subject as that of
Antonio Vivarini and
Giovanni d'Alemagna
at the Church of San
Pantalon. Beneath the
throne are putti who
hold up the instruments
of the Passion, while
below them are the
Evangelists flanked by
the four Doctors of the
Church. The surrounding
space is entirely occupied
by saints and orders
of angels.

24

33

25. Lorenzo Veneziano
(records from 1356 to 1372)

Polyptych Lion with the Annunciation

Panel, gold background, lower order: 126 × 75 cm (central), 121 × 60 cm (sides); upper order: 82 × 83 cm (central), 67 × 30 cm (eight sides), 35 × 5 cm (36 small panels on the pillars)
Acquisition: 1812, following the Napoleonic suppressions, (cat. 10)
Latest restoration: 1997

At left, the saints Anthony (Abbot), John the Baptist, Paul and Peter. At right, saints John the Evangelist, Magdalene, Dominic and Francis. On the upper order, the Holy Father giving his blessing among eight Prophets. Below, on the predella, are the hermit saints Saba, Macarius, Paul, Hilary and Theodore. A work of very high artistic quality, it was originally on the high altar of the now demolished Church of

1

34

Sant'Antonio in Castello. On the inscription on the tablets at the sides of the central panel are written the date when the work was begun (1357) and the dedication to the commissioner Domenico Lion, shown to the lower right of the Virgin. The lower order – with its great Gothic elegance – is arranged according to a chromatic crescendo which begins with the dark tones of the side figures of Saint Anthony and Saint Francis and gradually reaches full chromatic luminosity in the central scene of the Annunciation. The upper panel in the centre is a replacement of the original, which was lost, and is possibly the work of Benedetto Diana.

26d   26e   26f

26. Rimini School of the first half of the 14ᵗʰ century

Stories from the Passion of Christ and the Universal Judgement

Panel, gold background, 17 × 14 cm each
Acquisition: 1816, bequest of Girolamo Molin, (cat. 26)
Latest restoration: 1979

These panels belonged to the same group, together with the five panels of identical format in the Staatliche Museen, Berlin, and a *Deposition in the Tomb* in a private collection in Rome. The panels were probably the doors of a private devotional diptych with the Stories distributed on three registers.
More recently, the complex has been attributed to Giovanni Baronzio's early period.

27. Jacobello del Fiore and assistants (first half of the 15ᵗʰ century)

Coronation of the Virgin

Panel, gold background, 281 × 302 cm
Acquisition: 1882, by purchase from the Duomo of Cereda (cat. 1)
Latest restoration: 1994-95

Dates to the first half of the 15ᵗʰ century, the work was commissioned for Ceneda Cathedral by the city's bishop, Antonio Correr, who is depicted kneeling at the lower right. The crowded composition provides a more complex version of Guariento's *Paradise* in the Doge's Palace.

28. Jacopo Moranzone (records from 1430, died between 1467 and 1469)

Polyptych

Panel, gold background, 135 × 59 cm (central), 124 × 32 cm (sides)
Acquisition: 1812, following the Napoleonic suppressions, (cat. 11)
Latest restoration: 1952

On the central panel the *Assumption*; on the side panels Saints Helen, John the Baptist, Benedict and Elizabeth.
Originally in the Church of Sant'Elena, where it was painted with part of a bequest established in 1441 by Donna Elisabetta, the mother of Fra' Tommaso da Venezia. Sources indicate a possible inscription with the date of 1441, perhaps on the now lost wooden frame. Noted by Vasari in 1581 as the only work worthy of mention by the artist, who "made all his figures on the points

of their feet".
The Gothic-like composition, influenced by Michele di Matteo's polyptych for the same Church of Sant'Elena, indicates that the artist is barely aware of the new artistic ideas being developed in Venice at that time, while certain roughness around the edges reveal an aspect typical in engraving, which was an age old tradition in the Moranzone family.

27

28

The Great 15ᵗʰ Century Altarpieces and Giovanni Bellini

This room was constructed between 1886 and 1895 to house Titian's *Assumption* and other large altarpieces. After the *Assumption* was returned to the church of the Frari in 1919, the room appeared rather out of balance. To restore the room's harmony, Carlo Scarpa replaced the decorated ceiling with a dark green plaster, replaced the polychrome marble floor with a dark grey Venetian style *terrazzo*, and created a new stairway to Room 3.

Giovanni Bellini, Virgin Enthroned with Child, *detail*

1. **Vittore Carpaccio**
(Venice? c. 1460–before
1526)

*Crucifixion and the
Apotheosis of the 10,000
Martyrs of Mount Ararat*

Canvas, 311 × 204 cm
Acquisition: 1812
(cat. 89)

Signed and dated 1515,
painted for the Ottobon
altar in the demolished
Church of Sant'Antonio
di Castello. The
altarpiece was probably
commissioned by Ettore
Ottobon, the grandson
of the prior Francesco
Ottobon, who had ended
a plague at his monastery
by invoking the 10,000
martyrs of Mount Ararat.
9,000 Roman soldiers,
led by Acatio, were sent
against the Armenian
rebels and managed to
defeat them only after
an angel told them to
seek the help of Jesus,
who led them to Mount
Ararat, where he taught
them about the Christian
religion. Upon their
conversion, the emperor
approaches them
with other pagan kings,
threatening to make
them suffer the pains
endured by Jesus on the
Cross. Their firm faith,
even under torture,
led another 1,000
pagan soldiers to convert
and join up with the
new Christians.
During a violent storm,
a final passion occurs,
similar to that of Christ.
The altarpiece brings
various echoes together
of the more recent
contemporary culture
and, in spite of a certain
compositional virtuosity,
it constitutes an
extraordinary novelty
in the field of Venetian
religious painting.
In fact, it replaces
the usual votive
representation of one
or a few saints with
a plurality of images,
thereby depicting the
collectivity of Christian
virtue.

1

2. **Marco Basaiti**
(Venice
1470/75–after 1530)

*Prayer in the Garden with
Saint Mark, Saint Louis
of Toulose and Saint Francis*

Canvas for transport from
a panel, 369 × 222 cm
Acquisition: 1815
(cat. 69)
Latest restoration: 1987

At the foreground to the
left on the ground is the
fragmentary signature and
the date of 1510. The
altarpiece was originally
in the Church of San
Giobbe, on the first altar
to the right belonging to
the Foscari family. The
composition follows
a pyramidal scheme:
the evangelical event takes
place beyond the arc,
while at the front are
the eponymous saints
of the Foscari family
– Louis (Ludovic of
Toulouse) and Francis
to the left, Dominic
and Mark to the right –
presented as intermediaries
between the faithful and
the divinity.

2

3. **Giovanni Bellini**
(Venice 1434/39-1516)

Virgin Enthroned with Child between Saint Francis, Saint John the Baptist, Saint Job, Saint Domenic, Saint Sebastian, Saint Ludovic and Angels Playing Music; known as the *San Giobbe Altarpiece*

Panel, 471 × 292 cm
Acquisition: 1815
(cat. 38)
Latest restoration:
1994-95 and 2004

Originally in the Church of San Giobbe on the altar of Saint Job (Giobbe), the second one to the right. The large panel received great admiration from other artists at the time of its creation, and became a model for successive altarpieces. It has been shortened by 50 cm at the top. The presence of the apotropaic saints Sebastian and Roch indicates that the altarpiece was painted during a plague, probably the one of 1478. The niche, with its naturally proportioned figures composed in a pyramid, is almost a symbolic representation of the San Marco Basilica: the apse with the gilt mosaics, the stone wall panelling, the seraphs all allude to the Basilica. The triads of saints to the left and right of the Madonna are arranged in triangular patterns. In its original location, the illusion of depth was accentuated by sculpted pillars on the altar, faithful repetitions of those painted on the piece. The angels in the lower area playing the lute and the lyre honour Saint Job, the patron saint of music.

2

3

4. Vittore Carpaccio
(Venice? c. 1460 – 1525/26)

Presentation of Christ in the Temple

Panel, 420 × 231 cm
Acquisition: 1815, from the Church of San Giobbe, (cat. 44)
Latest restoration: 1995

Signed and dated 1510, the altarpiece was originally in the church of San Giobbe in the third altar on the right (dedicated to the Purification of the Virgin), and was probably commissioned by Pietro di Matteo Sanudo. The presentation of the infant Jesus in the temple – forty days after his birth – occurs in a space in the shape of an apse, whereas the figures are all composed in a pyramidal arrangement. In addition to the extraordinary chromatic quality – recovered with the most recent restoration – certain aspects bear emphasising: the female faces inspired by the works of Pietro Perugino; the scenes from *Genesis* and the *Apocalypse* decorating the clothes of Simon, the priest; the three angels at the base playing the lute, lyre and *cromocorno*.
Considered to be a preparatory study for the two women's heads to the left of the Virgin, is a drawing in the Ashmolean Museum, Oxford, which was also used for the *Apotheosis of Saint Ursula* (Room 21, cat. 576).

2

4

5. **Giambattista Cima da Conegliano**
(Conegliano 1459-1517)
Madonna of the Orange Tree between Saint Ludovic of Toulose and Saint Girolamo

Panel, 211 cm × 139 cm
Acquisition: 1919,
returned from Austria,
(cat. 815)
Latest restoration: 1995

This signed altarpiece was originally to the right of the high altar in the church of Santa Chiara on Murano, and belonged to Franciscan monks. The presence of the Franciscan saint Ludovic of Toulouse, and the two monks about to enter the woods suggest that the work was commissioned by the same order. The theme is a variation on the "Flight into Egypt", an allusion provided by Saint Joseph and the ass in the background. The *sacra conversazione* thus takes place in a wide landscape, where certain symbols of Mary can be recognised, such as the city on the hill which recalls the birthplace of the artist, and rock which is also Mary's throne, and the orange tree after which the painting was named. The work dates to between 1496 and 1498.

2

5

43

6. **Marco Basaiti**
(Venice 1470/75-post 1530)

Vocation of the Sons of Zebedee

Panel, 385 × 265 cm
Acquisition: 1812, following the Napoleonic suppressions, (cat. 39)
Latest restoration: 1990-91

Signed and dated Marco Basaiti 1510, the work was once on the high altar of the Church of Sant'Andrea della Certosa. The most recent restoration revealed that the altarpiece was enlarged when the work was almost complete with the addition of the boats and the fisherman (Mark 1, 16-20), also with some corrections to the large figures in the foreground and to the background. The work was probably begun by Alvise Vivarini, but when this master died it was taken over and completed by Marco Basaiti, who worked in Vivarini's workshop at that time. The evangelical theme of the 'calling' is a clear reference to monastic life, also alluded to in various other sybolic motifs in the composition.

6

7. **Giambattista Cima da Conegliano**
(Conegliano 1459-1517)

Doubting Thomas with Saint Magnus

Panel, 210 × 141 cm
Acquisition: 1829, following the Napoleonic suppressions, (cat. 611)
Latest restoration: 1998

From the Scuola dei Mureri (masons) at San Samuele, with the Scuola's patrons, the saints Thomas and Magnus the Bishop, also depicted. The work dates to around 1504-05, immediately after the London version of the same subject, carried out originally for a confraternity in Portogruaro between 1502 and 1504. The episode does not unfold in an enclosed space, as the evangelical tradition would normally have it, but in an open loggia, with Saint Magnus taking the place of the usual eleven apostles. The careful use of shadows and light and the extraordinary compositional balance make this one of the most important of the artist's works of that time.

7

2

8

8. **Giovanni Bellini**

and assistants
(Venice 1434/39–1516)

Mourning the Dead Christ

Canvas, 445 × 310 cm
Acquisition: 1829,
following the Napoleonic
suppressions (cat. 166)
Latest restoration: 1964

Originally in the now
demolished Church of
Santa Maria dei Servi on
one of the first altars on
the right, demolished in
1510 and reconstructed at
the expense of the Servite
friars. The painting also
dates to about that time,
and its very high quality – in spite of a previous
attribution to Rocco
Marconi – suggests that
Bellini was largely
responsible for the piece,
with only limited
intervention from his
assistants. St. Joseph
of Arimathea, the Virgin
and the Magdalen are
recognizable, but it is
harder to identify the two
figures at the ends.
Previously thought to be
St. Martha and St. Philip
Benizi, it has been
suggested more recently
that they are St. Juliana
Falconieri and St.
Bonaventure of Forli.

9. **Giambattista Cima da Conegliano**

(Conegliano 1459–1517)

Virgin with Child and Saints Catherine(?), George, Nicholas, Sebastian and Lucy(?)

Panel, 414 × 209 cm
Acquisition: 1812,
following the Napoleonic
suppressions (cat. 36)
Latest restoration: in
progress

From the chapel of San
Gregorio in the Church
of Santa Maria della
Carità. According to
sources, the marble frame
had been commissioned
from Cristoforo Solari of Milan by the
shipowner Giorgio
Dragan, probably
depicted in the
features of Saint
George. In the
original location,
the painting probably
presented a strong
spatial affinity
between its painted
architectural elements
and the actual
architectural
structures surrounding
it. The work was
probably completed
in around 1499, the
date of the very
similar polyptych
by Miglionico.

2

9

Giovanni Bellini, Giorgione, Cima da Conegliano, Sebastiano del Piombo and Diana

This room was originally part of the Scuola della Carità, but was later called the Canova Room because it once contained a porphyry urn with his right hand, now located in the *tablinum*.
The casings of the windows were designed by Carlo Scarpa, probably when he planned the adjacent rooms

Giovanni Bellini and assistants,
The Annunciation,
detail

1a

1b

1. Sebastiano Luciani, called 'del Piombo'
(Venice 1485–Rome 1547)

Saints Louis, Sinibald, Bartholomew and Sebastian

Canvases, 292 × 137 cm, 292 × 137 cm, 292 × 136 cm, 292 × 136 cm
Latest restoration: 1984–85

These were the external and internal doors of an organ (now destroyed) in the Church of San Bartolomeo, displayed here until a definitive restoration of the original location is completed. Inspired by Giovanni Bellini and Giorgione, the paintings date to around 1508-09 and constitute the most important commission for the young artist.

1c

1d

2. **Giambattista Cima da Conegliano**
(Conegliano 1459-1517)

Madonna and Child between the Baptist and Saint Paul

Panel, 82 × 114 cm
Acquisition: 1838, donated by Girolamo Contarini (cat. 603)
Latest restoration: 2005

Dates from the early years of the 16th century. The Virgin's face already displays traits typical of Cima's style, although the influence of Giovanni Bellini is still dominant.

3. **Giovanni Bellini**
and assistants
(Venice 1434/39-1516)

The Herald Angel, The Annunciation and Saint Peter

Canvas, 225 × 105 cm each
Acquisition: 1907, *The Angel* by purchase; 1910, *The Annunciation,* withdrawn from the depository of San Francesco della Vigna, 1908 by revocation of the deposit by the church of the Frari, *San Pietro* (cat. 734)
Latest restoration: 1998

The two paintings, representing the Annunciation, originally decorated the external doors of the organ of Santa Maria dei Miracoli; the internal doors had *Saint Peter* and a *Saint Paul* (lost). The work has been attributed to various artists, including Carpaccio, as an external reference to the *Dream of Ursula*; today it is believed to have been the work of some artists working in the style of Giovanni Bellini, and based on drawings by the master. The marble pieces in the painting recall those of the interior of the Church dei Miracoli, which was completed in 1489. This date signals the *post quem* period for the date of the paintings, which are probably from the last decade of that century.

3a

3b

3c

4

4. Giambattista Cima da Conegliano
(Conegliano 1459-1517)

Pietà

Panel, 70 × 113 cm
Acquisition: 1850,
bequest of Felicita Renier
(cat. 604)
Latest restoration: 1990

Signed bottom-right, the piece appears to be from the younger period of the artist's life (around 1490), as it has no landscape details whatsoever. The many allusions to Alvise Vivarini, Antonello and Giovanni Bellini combine to create a piece of great balance.

5. Sebastiano Luciani known as del Piombo
ascribed to
(Venice 1485-Rome 1547)

Virgin with Child, Saint Catherine and Saint John the Baptist

Panel, 51 × 80 cm
Acquisition: 1838,
donation from
Girolamo Contarini
(cat. 70)
Latest restoration: 2002

From the Contarini collection, the piece may have been commissioned by a certain Caterina Contarini, as the inclusion of Saint Catherine would indicate. Although critics are divided as to whether the painting is by Sebastiano del Piombo or by Giorgione (or one of his followers), the style of the painting recalls the early efforts of Sebastiano, characterised by the influence of Giovanni Bellini and the modern 'language' employed by Giorgione.

3

5

6. **Benedetto Rusconi, called 'Diana'**
(Venice 1460-Rome 1525)

The Virgin with Child and Saint John, Saint Louis and Saint Monica

Panel, 180 cm × 152 cm
Acquisition: 1832
Latest restoration: 1979
(cat. 86)

Originally on the altar of the sacristy in the Church of Maria dei Servi, where it was placed upon a lunette with the *Holy Father*, identified by some as the one set at the top of the large polyptych by Lorenzo Veneziano in Room 1. It is a late work from around 1520, when the influence of Giorgione was enriched by experience with contemporary Lombard painting.

6

7

7. **Giorgione**
(Castelfranco
c. 1476/77-
Venice 1510)

Nude

Detached fresco,
243 × 140 cm
Acquisition: 1937,
from the top storey
of the Fondaco dei
Tedeschi, front facing
onto the Grand Canal
Latest restoration:
1977

3

The fragment of the feminine figure usually defined "Nude", but in reality allegorical figure holding in hand a sphere, comes from the façade of the Fondaco dei Tedeschi, ended by Giorgione in 1508. It was part of a wide decoration which developed a complex iconographical programme, already unclear to Vasari (1568). In spite of the precarious preservative condition, it is possible to recognize the marks of the deep original tone.

Giovanni Bellini, Andrea Mantegna, Piero della Francesca, Cosmè Tura and Giorgione

Carlo Scarpa redesigned these two rooms (4 and 5) in 1955, walling over their windows and making them into one open space divided at the centre by a panel placed in correspondence with the two skylights that formerly occupied that spot. Works were shown using only original frames or frames of the same era; paintings which lacked a frame were inserted into wooden panels lined with material. For Giorgione's *Tempesta* an old brown velvet was used, the same one seen today.

Giorgione, La Tempesta, *detail*

4/5

3. Piero della Francesca
(Borgo San Sepolcro, 1416/17-1492)

Saint Jerome and a Devotee

Panel, 49 × 42 cm
Acquisition: 1850, bequest from Felicita Renier, (cat. 47)
Latest restoration: 1948

The artist's signature "*Pietri de bu/go sci sep/ulcri opus*" (a work of Pietro di Borgo San Sepolcro) can be seen on the trunk of the tree where the cross is mounted. Although he has none of the traditional attributes, the devotee kneeling before Saint Jerome was recognised by a later inscription as the Venetian Girolamo Amadi di Agostino, originally of Lucca. The work was originally for private devotion, and dates to around 1450. A new, more balanced rapport between saint and worshiper is evident here, with the devotee portrayed in natural proportions. The landscape shows the homeland of the painter, San Sepulcro, and the Tiber Valley (although all the green components have unfortunately turned brown).

1. Giovanni Bellini
(Venice 1434/39-1516)

Virgin with Child

Panel, 77 × 57 cm
Acquisition: 1812, following the Napoleonic suppressions, (cat. 583)
Latest restoration: 1938

Traditionally identified as the *Madonna* which was once in the Palazzo dei Camerlenghi, the treasurers of the Venetian State, at the Rialto, although there is no trace of the gold background which that piece supposedly had. The painting dates to the 1470s and already reveals some of the typical traits of many Bellini Madonnas, where the influence of Mantegna – the artist's brother-in-law – is softened by a new sense of spirituality and humanity.

2. Andrea Mantegna
(Isola di Cartura, Padua, 1431 – Mantua 1506)

Saint George

Panel, 66 × 32 cm
Acquisition: 1856, by purchase from the Manfrin collection, (cat. 588)
Latest restoration: 1992

Dated about 1446, this painting is believed to have been the side panel of a polyptych, but no confirmation of this has as yet been found. The stern young man – more mythical hero than Christian saint – wears a breast-plate inspired by a drawing of Jacopo Bellini, Mantegna's father-in-law. The fortified city in the background – also taken from a drawing by Jacopo – is a depiction of Selene, where according to the legend Saint George slew the dragon.

Jacopo Bellini
(records from
1424-1470/71)

4. *Virgin with Child*

Panel, 94 × 66 cm
Acquisition: 1829,
it is not known how
this work reached the
Galleries (cat. 582)
Latest restoration: 1979

This work, already in
Padua at the end of the
18th century, in the
possessions of Abbot
Foscarini, was then
acquired by the engraver
Sasso. It is signed on the
original frame. Dating
to around the 1450s, it
belongs to the mature
period of Jacopo Bellini,
father of Giovanni. The
heads of the cherubs are
also found in some
drawings by the artist in
a book at the Louvre.

5. *Virgin with Child*

Panel, 63 × 47 cm
Acquisition: 1920, by
purchase (cat. 835)
Latest restoration: 1994

The Madonna and the
Child are not painted
here in the traditional full
face manner of Byzantine
painting but rather at
a slight angle, and appear
to be engaged in a subtle
dialogue, an innovation
that places the work
in the mature period
of the artist's work.

3

4

5

6. Cosmè Tura
(Ferrara 1430-95)

Virgin with Child

Panel, 61 × 41 cm
Acquisition: 1896,
purchased, (cat. 628)
Latest restoration: 1982

A work by the master of the 15ᵗʰ century Ferrarese School of painting, dated between 1459 and 1463. This painting was probably conceived for a private residence, as the inscription near the bottom would indicate: "Sviglia el tuo figlio dolce madre pia / per far infin felice l'alma mia" ("Wake your sweet son, oh pious mother / and so make joyful my soul"). On the spandrel of the frame, two angels hold aloft the symbol of Saint Bernard, while the bunches of grapes with the goldfinches are symbols of the Passion of Christ. The small panel is also called *The Madonna of the Zodiac*, for the zodiacal signs traced in gold on the background; the signs for Acquarius, Pisces, Sagittarius and Virgo are still legible, while those to the right have all nearly disappeared. The presence of profane elements in a sacred painting, including references to astrology, reflects an intellectual custom of the time and is recurrent in Ferrarese painting.

4/5

6

Giovanni Bellini
(Venice 1434/39-1516)

7. Madonna Enthroned Cherishing the Sleeping Child

Panel, 63 × 120 cm
Acquisition: 1812, following the Napoleonic suppressions (cat. 591)
Latest restoration: 2000. Damaged at the top

The painting is from the Doge's Palace (Magistrate of the Militia of the Sea), and was perhaps the central part of a larger group. In this work of the 1470s, Bellini again reveals his attentive observation of the contemporary figurative culture: the pose of the Madonna resembles the one in the polyptych by Bartolomeo Vivarini (Room 23, cat. 615), while the throne motif is taken from the Mantegna altarpiece of San Zeno in Verona.

8. Virgin with Child and Saints Catherine and Magdalene

Panel, 107 × 58 cm
Acquisition: 1850, bequest of Felicita Renier, following the Napoleonic suppressions (cat. 613)
Latest restoration: 1997

Dated around 1500 (although some critics place it at about 10 years earlier), this painting reflects the influence of Leonardo da Vinci in its treatment of the relationship between background and subject, for example in how the side lighting makes the figures appear from the shadows. (In fact, Leonardo was in Venice during the 1500s, sketching the portrait of Isabella d'Este.) Adorned with jewels and dressed with refined elegance, the two saints seem more like two young Venetian patricians than celestial creatures. A workshop copy of this piece is on display in Prado museum, Madrid.

7

8

9. Hans Memling
(Selingestadt am Main c. 1440-Bruges 1494)

Portrait of a Young Man

Panel, 26 × 20 cm
Acquisition: 1856,
by purchase from the
Manfrin collection,
(cat. 586)
Latest restoration: 1998

The portrait of the young man with his hair arranged in the 'Italian' style is exemplary of Memling's portraiture. Viewed from a three-quarters perspective and cropped at the shoulders, he is supported to the right by an invisible parapet in front of a landscape with trees. His pensive mien is revealed by the frontal lighting, while the sober clothing appears black today, but was originally a dark reddish brown. The work dates to around 1480 or shortly thereafter.

Giovanni Bellini
(Venice 1434/39-1516)

10. *Virgin with Child and Saints Paul and George*

Panel, 65 × 88 cm
Acquisition: 1850,
bequest from Felicita
Renier (cat. 610)
Latest restoration: 2000

In this work, which dates from the last decade of the 1400s, the artist varies the "Virgin with Child" theme derived from the well-known *Madonna degli Alberetti*; he wides the format, making it more horizontal, and inserted the two saints. Comparison with the head of Saint Paul in the *Coronation* in Pesaro reveals how the artist is now seeking a softer form. In spite of the expressive strength of Saint George – perhaps a portrait of the commissioner – and the compositional innovations, the work was probably completed with the help of assistants.

9

11. *Virgin with Child, John the Baptist and a Saint*

Panel, 55 × 77 cm
Acquisition: 1926, from the Giovanelli collection by special agreement with the State (cat. 881)
Latest restoration: 1998

The work attests to the artist's attempt at the beginning of the 1500s to insert figures taller than the usual half-bust into a more articulated space. It also reveals numerous corrections over the course of the painting. The gestures, the poses and the expressions of the images in the foreground

10

prefigure the Passion of the baby Jesus, depicted with his feet already crossed, just as they will be on the cross. The landscape in the background is full of Marian symbols such as the castle, the port, the fortress and the mountains, which – together with the christological elements – were intended to provoke the devout oration of the faithful.

12. Pietà

Panel, 65 × 87 cm
Acquisition: 1934, from the Donà delle Rose collection, following a convention, (cat. 883)
Latest restoration: 1996

A work commissioned for private use, Bellini's Pietà dates to the beginning of the 16th century and is signed near the bottom on the left side. It originally belonged to the Martinengo family who had it restored in 1866. The most recent

restoration revealed the well preserved paint. Careful analysis of the meadow and the image of Mary holding her dead Son suggest the influence of Dürer, or in any case of Flemish culture. Rich with religious symbolism (including the dry tree

covered in ivy and the small shrub to the left of Christ, symbols of Judaism and Christianity), the background landscape brings together buildings of various origin in suggestive synthesis, including the pre-Palladian basilica, the

duomo and the tower of Vicenza, a view of the Natisone at Cividale and the bell tower of Sant'Appollinare at Ravenna.

4/5

13

14

Giovanni Bellini
(Venice 1434/39-1516)

13. *Madonna of the Red Cherubs*

Panel, 77 × 60 cm
Acquisition: 1812
(cat. 612)
Latest restoration: 1995

From the late 1400s, this work was originally in the Scuola della Carità. The motif of the red cherubs, burning with love, is taken from the Pesaro *Coronation* of 1474. In the background – a luminous landscape rich with Marian symbols such as the hills, the river and the fortified city – Mary regards her Son, almost enclosed in her hands, with tender awareness of his destiny.

14. *Madonna of the Alberetti (Madonna of the Trees)*

Panel, 71 × 58 cm
Acquisition: 1938, donated by Girolamo Contarini.
(cat. 596)
Latest restoration: 1997

The first dated work by Giovanni Bellini (the date 1487 and Bellini's

signature can be seen near the bottom in the centre, almost as if the foot of the small Jesus were pointing to them). The two trees at the side, for which the piece is named, may allude to the *Song of Songs*, or rather, given the dry shrubs at the sides of the trees, to the Old and New Testament. The luminosity of the thin bands of landscape, the play between shadows and light, and the posture of the Mother allowing the devotee to observe her Son – barely covered her delicate hands – make this is one of the most moving works for private devotion.

15. *Virgin with Child*

Panel, 60 cm × 78 cm
Acquisition: 1838, by donation from Girolamo Contarini (cat. 594)
Latest restoration: 2000

This may be the same *Madonna* that Taddeo Contarini left to his relative Girolamo in his will of 1578. Dating to 1480, the piece was created for private

devotion and was copied in many variations by the master's collaborators; Giovanni himself would refer back to it some years later in his *Madonna degli Alberetti*.
In the background can be seen the Torre di

Piazza in Vicenza, as it appeared to people arriving from Venice and Padua.

15

Giorgione
(Castelfranco 1476/77-
Venice 1510)

16. *La Vecchia*
(The Old Woman)

Canvas, transferred
from previous canvas,
68 × 59 cm
Acquisition: 1856,
by acquisition from
the Manfrin collection,
(cat. 272)
Latest restoration: 1984

Like the *Tempesta*, *La*
Vecchia was also part of the
Vendramin collection, and
is quoted in its inventory
of 1567-69 and 1601.
The entry for 1601 also
provides a measurement
of the frame, which is still
the original one. It was
later acquired by the
merchant Cristoforo
Orsetti, who mentions it
in his last will and
testament of 1664
(Borean-Mason), and was
inherited by his son
Giovan Battista. At an
unknown date it entered
the Manfrin collection.
The interpretation of this
work is extremely
controversial: clearly an
allegory, judging by the
inscription "in time"
on the scroll, it is also,
quite apart from any
symbolism, an
extraordinary portrait.
Dating to after 1505,
it seems to reflect certain
ideas of Leonardo da
Vinci, evident in the dark
background, the impious
analysis, but without
turning into caricature,
the gesture of the hand
pointed towards the chest,
similar to that of the
apostle Philip in da Vinci's
Last Supper in Milan.

16

17

17. Giorgione

(Castelfranco 1476/77–
Venice 1510)

La Tempesta

Canvas, 82 × 73 cm
Acquisition: 1932,
purchased from Prince
Alberto Giovanelli
(cat. 915)
Latest restoration: 1984

This painting has always
been identified with
"el paeseto in tela con la
tempesta con la cingana
et soldato, fu de man
de Zorzi di Castelfranco"
("the landscape on canvas
with the gypsy and soldier
in a storm, by the hand
of Giorgione of
Castelfranco"), mentioned

in 1530 by the historian
Marcantonio Michiel in
Gabriele Vendramin's
"camerino delle anticaglie"
(cabinet of antiques).
It is also indicated in an
inventory for Vendramin's
heirs in 1567-69, and in
another in 1601. It was
subsequently purchased
by the wealthy merchant
Cristoforo Orsetti
(Borean-Mason), who refers
to it in his will of 1664.
Left to his son Salvatore,
it ended up in the hands
of Girolamo Manfrin at the
end of the 18th century. Its
presence in his collection
was recorded by writers
and travelers from the
beginning of the 19th

century onward. In 1875
it was acquired by Prince
Giovannelli. Then there is
no mention of the piece
until 1855, when it is
recorded in the Manfrin

palazzo before passing on to
Prince Giovanelli in 1875.
X-ray and IR analyses have
revealed a nude woman
seated below the young man,
washing herself in the pool

18a

18b

of water to the left, and numerous other small corrections, especially in the landscape. A work for private enjoyment, the *Tempesta* has been the source of countless interpretations, from mythological to allegorical and even political. It has also been seen as the melding of many literary and figurative sources, or even as a work which would not require any decoding whatsoever, representing simply what Michiel has suggested: a "tempest" with a gypsy. The dating of the piece is also controversial, although it should be around 1505.

Giovanni Bellini
(Venice 1434/39–1516)
18. *Scroll and Head of Christ*
Panel, 33 × 22 cm
Acquisition: 1838, donation from Girolamo Contarini (cat. 87)
Latest restoration: 1994

The two fragments (the signature appears on the second one) were probably part of a *Transfiguration* or *Ascension*. There used to be a painting of the same subject by the artist in the chapel in Vicenza Cathedral once dedicated to the *Transfiguration*, but it has now been lost. A new kind of humanity can be seen in the face of Christ, bringing it closer to the *Baptism* in Santa Corona, Vicenza, in the early 1500s.

19. *Allegorical scenes*
Panels, 27 × 19 cm, 34 × 22 cm, 34 × 22 cm, 34 × 22 cm, 34 × 22 cm
Acquisition: 1838 (cat. 595)
Latest restoration: 2000

Dating from the early 1500s, the panels were probably part of a piece of furniture with a mirror, used for holding toiletries. These were so popular as to attract the attention of the Senate, which prohibited their construction in 1479. The images that decorated the pieces were moral allegories. The woman with the sphere is perhaps a

depiction of Melancholy or fickle Fortune; the nude with the mirror represents Vanity, and the reflection may be of the commissioner; the image of Bacchus on a chariot offering a plate of fruit to a warrior is a reference to Lust, tempting the virtuous man; the allegory of Slander or Envy is represented by the panel with a seashell and a man with a twisted snake. The first panel – which was probably part of a different piece, or a replacement of a lost part – has been attributed to Andrea Previtali (Bergamo 1470/80-1528). It depicts blindfolded Fortune, set between two spheres, with two amphoras containing pleasure and anguish. This iconography was common in the Germanic tradition.

19a

19b

19e

19c

4/5

19d

19e

Titian, Jacopo Tintoretto and Paolo Veronese

Part of the "*Nuovissima*" (very new) room connecting the old Scuola with Rooms 9 and 11, this room and the neighbouring rooms were built between 1840 and 1857. For a long time this was one of the poorest rooms in the Galleries, but in 1988, when the exhibition was held of Paolo Veronese's restored works, it was here that some of his great ceiling paintings were housed.

Two walled-up windows facing onto Palladio's front were reopened over the course of 2000.

Veronese,
Venice Receiving Gifts
from Hercules and Ceres,
detail

1. Titian (Tiziano Vecellio)
(Pieve di Cadore c. 1488/90-Venice 1576)

Saint John the Baptist

Canvas, 201 × 119 cm
Acquisition: 1808
(cat. 314)
Latest restoration: 1981

Signed "Ticianus" on the stone at the bottom, this painting was originally located in the church of Santa Maria Maggiore and after strong protest from the Venetians, the piece was entrusted to the Galleries rather than being transferred to the Brera gallery in Milan. The work follows a precise figurative programme in which "drawing", "colour" and "invention" are merged – almost a response to the Tuscan debate over whether Venetian artists were incapable of drawing well. The figure of the saint – whose stunning preparatory sketch has been revealed by the reflectography – recalls both Michelangelo and classical art sources, while the background landscape is decidedly fresh and new. The work is from around the time of the *Presentation of Mary at the Temple* (Room 24, cat. 626), and the *Christ Crowned with Thorns* in the Louvre, which date to 1540.

Jacopo Robusti, called 'Tintoretto'
(Venice 1519-1594)

2. *The Creation of the Animals*

Canvas, 150 × 258 cm
Acquisition: 1928, from the depository of the Doge's Palace (cat. 900)
Latest restoration: 1967

3. *The Temptation of Adam and Eve*

Canvas, 150 × 220 cm
Acquisition: 1812, following the Napoleonic suppressions (cat. 43)
Latest restoration: 1967

4. *Cain and Abel*

Canvas, 149 × 196 cm
Acquisition: 1812, following the Napoleonic suppressions (cat. 41)
Latest restoration: 1967

These three works were created between 1550 and 1553 and were originally in the Scuola della Trinità, a school instituted by the Teutonic Knights near the Dogana da Mar, which was demolished in the 1600s for the construction of the Salute Basilica and rebuilt nearby. There were originally five paintings with the Stories of Genesis which were to complete the decoration of the Albergo Room, begun by Francesco Torbido. Of the five canvases by Tintoretto in addition to these, there is a fragment with *Adam and Eve before the Holy Father* at the Uffizi in Florence. On the *Creation*, the articulate forms of the other two stories becomes a painting composed almost like a tapestry, where a single vital breath seems to animate the Creator and his creatures. On the *Adam and Eve*, the nude bodies – arranged diagonally according to a refined mannerist technique – rake against the dense mass of foliage. Adam and Eve are captured just before the consummation of their sin; to the right the sin

6

1

2

has already been
committed and the two
progenitors are chased
out by the angel.
This is a fundamental
work for the artist's
treatment of landscapes.
Also on *Cain and Abel*
the figures are depicted
against dense vegetation,
which opens to the right
onto an extraordinary
piece of landscape,
with the minuscule figure
of Cain wandering
in the distance. The scene
recalls a similar subject
by Andrea Schiavone
in the Galleria Palatina
in Florence, and especially
the Titian painting
of the ceiling of Santo
Spirito in Isola, later
transferred to the sacristy
of the Salute Basilica.

3

4

5

6

5. **Jacopo Robusti, called 'Tintoretto'**
(Venice 1519-1594)

Saint Louis, Saint George and the Princess

Canvas, 230 × 150 cm
Acquisition: 1937,
from the Ante-Chiesetta
room at the Doge's Palace
where it had been stored
(cat. 899)
Latest restoration: 1986

Like the *Saints Jerome and Andrew*, this work was created for the first room of the Salt Magistrate in the Palazzo Camerlenghi at the Rialto, and was commissioned by the magistrates Giorgio Venier

and Alvise Foscarini who, upon completion of their service on September 13, 1551 and May 1, 1552, offered a votive painting for their office. The work was completed around 1552. On the composition, with its anti-conformist and unusual iconography, the female figure ardently rides the dragon in a posture of great virtuosity, turned round towards the back and towards the saviour, mirroring herself in his bright breastplate. Saint Louis' pensive aspect comprises a very effective scene. Tintoretto probably

had some contact with contemporary theatre, and it may even be the case that he took inspiration from the set of Aretino's *Talanta*, drawn by Vasari around 1542.

6. *Saints Jerome and Andrew*

Canvas, 230 × 150 cm
Acquisition: 1937, from the Ante-Chiesetta at the Doge's Palace, where it had been stored (cat. 898)
Latest restoration: 1986

The painting was commissioned by the magistrates Andrea Dandolo and Girolamo

Bernardo, who completed their service on September 6, 1552 and October 9, 1552. This last date provides us with a *post quem* date for the completion of the work, which was painted shortly after *Saint Louis, Saint George and the Princess*. The large cross painted transversally between the two nude bodies of the saints creates the optical illusion of extraordinary depth.

7. **Paolo Caliari, called 'Veronese'**
(Verona 1528-Venice 1588)

Venice Receiving Gifts from Hercules and Ceres

Canvas, 308 × 327 cm
Acquisition: 1895, from Palazzo Reale (cat. 45)
Latest restoration: 1986

Originally on the ceiling of the Corn Magistrate's room in the Doge's Palace, in 1792 it was brought to the Marciana Library. In 1810 it was moved to the ceiling of the Napoleonic wing, and then later to the Accademia. The format of the painting, perhaps rectangular originally, was altered, probably in conjunction with its first transfer. It dates to around the same time as the canvases in the Collegio room of the Doge's Palace, and especially *Venice with Justice and Peace* of 1576-78. A fundamental work of the artist for its crafted use of perspective and counter lighting and its chromatic refinement.

6

7

69

8

**Paolo Caliari,
called 'Veronese'**
(Verona 1528-Venice 1588)

8. *San Francesco Receiving
the Stigmata*

Canvas, 256 × 432 cm
Acquisition: 1919,
returned from Austria
(cat. 833)
Latest restoration: 1986

9. *Saint Nicholas,
Recognised as the Bishop
of Myra*

Canvas, diam. 200 cm
(cat. 661)
Acquisition: 1817
Latest restoration: 1986

These paintings originally
decorated both the
ceiling of the demolished
church of San Nicolò
della Lattuga at the Frari,
together with the
Adoration of the Magi at
the centre and the four
Evangelists at the corners
(these five paintings are
now on the ceiling of the
chapel of the Rosary
at the church of Santi
Giovanni e Paolo. The
San Nicolò painting was
once rectangular, but like
Saint Francis was made
circular to be set in the
central space of the
ceiling of the first room
of the Galleries. The two
canvases represent the

artist's style in the 1580s,
incorporating a darker
palette in spite of the airy
depths furrowed by light
clouds, and significant
attention to perspective.
The paintings were
completed near the
re-consecration of the
church, which took place
in 1582.

10. **Paolo Caliari,
called 'Veronese',**
and assistants
(Verona 1528-Venice 1588)

Assumption of the Virgin

Canvas, 464 × 310 cm
Acquisition: 1818-21,
(cat. 541)
Latest restoration: 1988

The large canvas
decorated the ceiling
of the refectory of the
now demolished San
Giacomo convent on
Giudecca, flanked
by two ovals with the
Annunciation and the
Visitation (in storage),
and surrounded by a
frieze with leaves, putti
and figures. On the back
panel is the *Feast at the
House of Levi* (stored at
the Verona City Hall),
probably by Benedetto
Caliari. Although this is a
late work, and a
collaboration – as is

indicated by various
sources – Paolo is surely
responsible for much
of the actual painting
of the piece, and
the scenic creation with
the mannerist arbour,
which has its origins
in works by Correggio
or Parmigiannino.

11. **Paolo Caliari,
called 'Veronese'**
(Verona 1528-Venice 1588)

Coronation of the Virgin

Canvas, 405 × 219 cm
Acquisition: 1812
(cat. 264)
Latest restoration: 1969

Originally the altarpiece
of the high altar of the
Church of Ognissanti in
Venice which was
consecrated on July 21,
1586, the date which
should also correspond
to when the painting was
completed. One of the

9

6

70

artist's later works (elaborated on a sketch preserved at the Christ Church in Oxford), which critics have recently held to be almost entirely the work of the artist himself. The coronation of Mary is not a part of the evangelical tradition, but was a very diffuse devotional element at the popular level. The Virgin is crowned by the Holy Trinity in the presence of angelic choirs, the Evangelists, Apostles and all the saints, to whom the church was of course dedicated ("Ognissanti", "All Saints").

12. *Penitent San Jerome*

Canvas, 253 × 168 cm
Acquisition: Sant'Andrea della Zirada
Latest restoration: 1988

Stored at the Church of Sant'Andrea della Zirada, which was closed in 1971. Originally it was to the right of the high altar. This painting also belongs to the mature phase of the artist's work, as revealed by the beautifully rendered nude and the quality of the wide landscape to the right of the saint's home, identified with the usual attributes: the domesticated lion, the crucifix, the skull, the books, the cardinal's hat hung on the trunk. Dating to the end of the 1570s, this is the latest example of a theme treated by Paolo in 1566 for the church of Santa Maria degli Angeli on Murano (now at San Pietro Martire), and on a painting at the National Gallery in Washington.

10

11

6

12

Lorenzo Lotto, Savoldo, Romanino
and Jacopo Palma il Vecchio

Along with Room 6, these two rooms and the following, now used
as a sales outlet, are part of the "*Nuovissima*" (very new) wing of the
Galleries that was constructed between 1845 and 1875.
The rooms were remodelled by Carlo Scarpa in 1949. Prior to this,
in 1933, Room 7 was lined in green velvet and had been reserved
for two works by Giorgione: the famous *Tempesta*, and the *Nude*,
a fragment of the Fonte dei Tedeschi frescos, today on display in the
Galleria G. Franchetti at Ca' d'Oro. Scarpa added some false walls
to the room, thus creating a slightly trapezoid layout.

Lorenzo Lotto,
Portrait of a Gentleman
in his Study, *detail*

1. **Giovanni Busi, known as 'Cariani'**
(Venice, 1485/90–still living in 1547)

Portrait of a Man

Canvas, 68 × 56 cm
Acquisition: 1850, bequest from Felicita Renier, (cat. 299)

Completed around 1517, this portrait recalls the Giorgione-influenced culture in its use of colour, and in the expression and pose of the subject.

2. **Antonio Badile**
(Verona 1518–1560)

Portrait of Friar Salvo Avanzi

Canvas, 65 × 57 cm
Acquisition: 1957, by purchase option, (cat. 1318)
Latest restoration: 1958

This portrait, influence by Lotto, is signed and dated on the back "M. D. XXX. XVI." It depicts Avanzi with the attitude and symbols of Saint Thomas Aquinas, whose Dominican order the friar belonged to.

3. Giovanni Girolamo Savoldo

(Orzinuovi? 1480–c. 1550)

Saints Anthony Abbot and Paul the Hermit

Panel, 165 × 137 cm
Acquisition: 1856, purchase from the Manfrin collection, (cat. 328)
Latest restoration: 1997

On the stone at the bottom is the signature and date, perhaps decipherable as 1520. It is the first dated work of the painter, who appears to have been aware of the innovations of the Tuscan painters and the texts of Dürer and Leonardo da Vinci, but where an almost pre-Caravaggio Lombard element is particularly noticeable.

4. Alessandro Bonvicino, known as 'Moretto'

(Brescia 1498-1554)

Saint John the Baptist and Saint Peter

Panels, 114 × 50 cm, 113 × 51 cm
Acquisition: 1856, by purchase from the Manfrin collection, (cat. 332, 331)
Latest restoration: 1959

Early works, whose chromatic scheme and silvery coldness reveal the artist's Lombard origins, although enriched by his experience in Venice.

Bernardino Licinio

(Poscante c. 1490-Venice c. 1565)

5. Portrait of a Lady

Canvas, 68 × 60 cm
Acquisition: 1850, bequest from Felicita Renier, (cat. 303)

At the base, the two coats of arms with lions holding up the sun and the moon, belong perhaps to the Morello family of Treviso. From the 1540s, the portrait appears to imitate Paris Bordon's studies in colour and form.

6. Portrait of a Lady

Canvas, 47 × 45 cm
Acquisition: 1838, donation from Girolamo Contarini, (cat. 305)

A fine example of 16th century portraiture, this work is characterised by a warm tonality and studied psychological introspection.

4a   4b

5

6

7

7. **Lorenzo Lotto**
(Venice c. 1480–Loreto
1556)

*Portrait of a Gentleman
in his Study*

Canvas, 97 × 110 cm
Acquisition: 1930,
purchased (cat. 912)
Latest restoration: 1997

Painted between 1528 and
1530, this is one of the
most famous portraits by
Lotto. The young
melancholic man is
captured as a thought
distracts him from his
reading; his pallid face
emerging from the
darkness reveals a
psychological intensity
that foreshadows modern
portraiture. On the table,
the rose petals, ring, letters
and small lizard probably
allude to the transience
of life, and perhaps to an
unhappy and lost love.

Jacopo Negretti, known as 'Palma il Vecchio'
(Serina near Bergamo 1480-Venice 1528)

8. *Assumption of the Virgin*

Panel, 192 × 137 cm
Acquisition: 1812, following the Napoleonic suppressions (cat. 315)
Latest restoration: 1993

From the Scuola di Santa Maria Maggiore. The painter received 50 ducats on February 5, 1513 for this piece. Two episodes are depicted on it: the Assumption of the Virgin and the legend of the waistband that she will give to Thomas as proof of her rise to heaven. The Mary we see here is not extended upwards, but rather turned in a human gesture towards the small figure of the Apostle coming towards the mount to witness the event.

9. *Holy Family with Saint Catherine and Saint John the Baptist*

Canvas, 126 × 195 cm
Acquisition: 1900, by purchase (cat. 147)
Latest restoration: 1956

One of Palma's masterpieces, which remained unfinished at his death but was brought to completion by Titian, who painted the head of the saint and the landscape with the castle and pillar behind the Virgin, as analysis under infrared and ultraviolet light has shown.

7/8

8

9

10

11

10. **Titian**
(attributed)
(Pieve di Cadore
1488/90–Venice 1576)

Raphael the Archangel and Tobias

Panel, 170 × 149 cm
Acquisition: 1812
(cat. 1325)
Latest restoration: 1994

From the church of Santa Caterina. Below at the centre is the Bembo coat of arms. Cleaning has brought to light the extraordinary quality of the work, leading recent critics to suggest that the work was painted by Titian.

Bonifacio De' Pitati, called 'Bonifacio Veronese'
(Verona 1487–Venice 1553)

11. *The Eternal Father and Piazza San Marco*

Canvas, 165 × 130 cm
Acquisition: after 1808
(cat. 917)
Latest restoration: 1991

Originally the piece was the central part of a triptych, which the *Herald Angels* at the sides and the *Annunciation* (on display in the Quadreria) from the Camerlenghi Palazzo at the Rialto. The presence of the Loggetta of the campanile – completed by Sansovino in 1540 – provides a *post quem* date for the work, which is from around 1543-44. The view of San Marco reveals certain particulars of a slice of Venetian life: at the fore to the left a furrier's, near the campanile a group of acrobats, and in front the porters.

13a

13b

12

12. The Madonna of the Tailors

Canvas, 129 × 149 cm
Acquisition: 1945, from
Palazzo Reale (cat. 1305)

Signed and dated 1533, the work was originally on the altar of the Scuola dei Sartori (Tailors' School), with its symbol of a large scissors, here depicted at the feet of the Virgin. To the left, Omobono, the protector saint of the tailors, gives alms to a cripple: it is a clear message of charity to the more wealthy members of the Scuola.

13. Giorgio Vasari
(Arezzo 1511-Florence 1574)

Justice
Panel, 77 × 185 cm

Putto with Scroll
Panel, 77 × 65 cm

Putto with Scroll
Panel, 77 × 65 cm

Patience
Panel, 77 × 65 cm
Acquisition: 1987, by purchase (cat. 1370, 1372, 1373, 1371),
Latest restoration: 1989/90

These paintings come from the ceiling of the Palazzo Corner Spinelli on the Grand Canal. The decoration was completed in 1542 and included nine paintings (such as the allegorical figures of Faith, Hope and Charity); the first two are now in private collections in London, while the third, which ended up in Brera, was placed on deposit at the Galleries in 2002. The putti with scrolls are inspired by high-reliefs presently at the Archaeological Museum,

but which were once on the walls of a building in Piazza San Marco. The figures are cut projecting out from an invisible parapet against the depths of heaven, perfecting an idea of Pordenone on the lost ceiling of the Scuola di San Francesco at the Frari. This work attracted considerable attention from Venetian artists, particularly Paolo Veronese.

13c

13d

14a

14b

14. Andrea Previtali
(Barbenno, Bergamo
1470/80-Bergamo 1528)

Nativity

Canvas, 132 × 215 cm

Crucifixion

Canvas, 132 × 215 cm
Acquisition: 1897,
by exchange from the
Church of the Redentore
(cat. 639, 640)
Latest restoration: 1982

Dating to between 1515
and 1520, these early
paintings were perhaps
originally in the Doge's
Palace. The admiration
for Giovanni Bellini and
Lorenzo Lotto is evident.

**15. Girolamo Romani,
called 'Romanino'**
(Brescia 1484/87-c. 1556)

Deposition

Panel, 183 × 185 cm
Acquisition: 1909,
by purchase (cat. 737)
Latest restoration: 1975

An early work, signed
and dated 1510, originally
in the Church of San
Lorenzo in Brescia.
In addition to the
important elements taken
from Bellini, Giorgione
and Titian, there are also
significant Lombard
components, which
in their entirety form
a balanced synthesis
of form and colour.

**16. Sebastiano Luciani
called 'del Piombo' (?)**
(Venezia 1485 - Roma 1547)

Visitation

Canvas, 209 × 150 cm
Acquisition: 1814 (cat.
95)
Latest restoration: 2004

Originally in the
monastery of Sant'Andrea,
this work was attributed to
many of the great masters
of 16th century Venice. The
current restoration, while
revealing the lacunas, has
rendered more plausible its
attribution to the young
Sebastiano del Piombo,
around the time of the
Sacre Conversazioni in the
Louvre and in the
Metropolitan Museum.

15

16

Titian, Jacopo Tintoretto and Paolo Veronese

Begun by Francesco Lazzari in 1828, the room was inaugurated in 1834. The passage between this room and its twin hall (Room 11) is decorated with four columns in Greek marble from the Scuola di Santa Maria della Misericordia.

Titian, Pietà, *detail*

1

Paolo Caliari, known as 'Veronese'
(Verona 1528–Venice 1588)

1. *Virgin with Child and Saints*

Canvas, 338 × 187 cm
Acquisition: 1817,
following the Napoleonic
suppressions, (cat. 37)
Latest restoration: 1969–70

Originally on the altar of
the sacristy of the church
of San Zaccaria, the work
was taken to Paris in
1797 and then given to
the Accademia in 1815 in
exchange for three
paintings which are still
in the church. In 1562
Francesco Bonaldo
undertook to pay 200
ducats to refit the sacristy
and the altarpiece should
date to slightly later,
around 1564. The artist
appears particularly
interested in the
relationship with the
environment where the
painting was originally
kept, an aspect which is
of course now lost. The
mannerist elements
present here work
harmoniously and with
an almost classical sense
of balance, evidence that
Veronese had taken in the
great devotional tradition
of the 15th and 16th
centuries explored by
artists from Giovanni
Bellini to Titian.

2. *Christ in the House of Levi*

Canvas, 560 × 1309 cm
Acquisition: 1815,
following the Napoleonic
suppressions, (cat. 203)
Latest restoration: 1980–82

This great painting,
which was taken to Paris

3

and then returned in 1815, was originally a *Last Supper* for the refectory of the convent of Santi Giovanni e Paolo, as a replacement for a *Last Supper* by Titian which had been lost in a fire. According to the writing at the base of the pillar bottom left, the work was completed on April 20, 1573, but three months later the artist was accused of heresy for this vast composition which contained what were considered to be excessive anti-conformist elements. In spite of his strong defence of his artistic freedom, Veronese was ordered to "correct" the painting at his own expense within three months. But the only change he made was to

add the writing on the top of the pillar with the date below, clearly at the suggestion of Dominican scholars: "fecit D. Covi Magnum Levi – Luca Cap.V", so as to avoid scandal. In fact, Luke says in chapter V of his Gospel: "Levi held a great banquet for the Lord". In the work, with its triple-arch background inspired by the buildings of Palladio and Sansovino, Veronese's research into the idea of the banquet is concluded, with the attainment of a complete balance of scenic elements and figures.

3. *Allegory of the Battle of Lepanto*

Canvas, 170 × 137 cm
Acquisition: 1812, following the Napoleonic suppressions, (cat. 212)
Latest restoration: 1983

Originally in the Church of San Pietro Martire on Murano, to the right of the Rosary altar, while to the left was the *Madonna of the Rosary*, dated 1573 (Quadreria cat. 207), completed by the workshop based on a Veronese drawing. In the lower area is depicted the battle of Lepanto of 1571, which was between the Lega Santa and the Turkish Fleet, which was also commemorated by prints at around that time. On the upper part is Venice between Saint

Mark and Saint Giustina, on whose feast day the battle took place. Venetia is shown being presented to the Virgin, while to the left Saint Peter and Saint Roch intercede for her. The small canvas, clearly by the artist himself, was perhaps commissioned in 1573 as an *ex voto* by Pietro Giustinian of Murano, who had distinguished himself in the battle, or by Onfrè Giustinian who brought news of the victory to Venice.

2

Jacopo Robusti known as 'Tintoretto'
(Venice 1519-1594)

4. Transport of the Body of Saint Mark

Canvas, 397 × 315 cm
Acquisition: 1920, from the Salone Sansoviniano of the Libreria Marciana, (cat. 631)
Latest restoration: 1991-92

Painted between 1562 and 1566 for the Scuola Grande di San Marco (where the three paintings below are also from, while a find one with the *Discovery of the Body of Saint Mark* is in the Brera gallery in Milan), paid for by the Guardian Grande Tommaso Rangone. The

work attests to Tintoretto's extraordinarily imaginative and evocative style, and reveals the new *luminismo* which typifies Tintoretto's paintings from this period.

5. Miracle of Saint Mark Freeing a Slave

Canvas, 416 cm × 544 cm

Acquisition: 1821, with the works returned to Venice from Paris, (cat. 42)
Latest restoration: 1965

This was the first painting made by Tintoretto for the Chapter Hall of the Scuola Grande di San Marco. Brought to Paris in 1797, it was returned in 1815 and

10

4

entrusted to the Accademia Galleries. It was probably commissioned in 1547 and completed by April of 1548, when Aretino praised the work in a letter to Tintoretto. The scene is of a condemned slave being freed as a result of the intercession of Saint Mark. The slave was to be blinded and have his legs broken because – against the wishes of his master – he had gone to worship the relics of the saint. In this work, with its remarkable new dramatic effect and intense use of colour, the various figurative phases of the artist are summarised, especially the Michaelangelo-influenced aspects, rendered through a methodical graphic effort, in a vision of such newness that it could only provoke wonder and bewilderment from his contemporaries.

6. *Rescue at Sea*

Canvas, 396 × 334 cm
Acquisition: 1920, from the Salone sansoviniano of the Libreria Marciana, (cat. 832)
Latest restoration: 1992-93

Painted between 1562 and 1566, this painting depicts the miraculous rescue of a Saracen sailor who at the turn of Alexandria had called upon the saint during a storm. The painting is composed of two pieces which reveal transparent pencil sketches on the back, with no relation to the final composition but which indicate how Tintoretto used different fragments of canvas. This work is especially fascinating for its dramatic rendering of the turbulent seas and the extremely adept use of contrasts in light.

7

The invention of the angel who appears before the sleeping Mark, was doubtless the work of Domenico.

8. Jacopo Robusti, known as 'Tintoretto'
(Venice 1519-1594)

Virgin with Child and Saints Cecilia, Marina, Cosma and Damian

Canvas, 341 × 251 cm
Acquisition: 1812, following the Napoleonic suppressions, (cat. 221)
Latest restoration: 1991-92

This piece was originally on the first altar on the left in the Church of Santi Cosma e Damiano on the island of Giudecca. It dates to the 1550s. The chromatic alteration of the once much lighter large clouds is unfortunately irreversible.

9. Paolo Caliari (Veronese)
(Verona 1528-Venice 1588)

The Marriage of Saint Catherine

Canvas, 377 × 241 cm
Acquisition: 1918, taken back after the First World War from the church of S. Caterina, became State property following the Napoleonic suppressions, (cat. 1324)
Latest restoration: 1986

Painted for the high altar of the Venetian church of Santa Caterina.
The painting was taken from the church during the World War I.
The emphasis is by now pre-Baroque, with its extraordinary chromatic elements and serene beauty of the images.
The piece was very well received by contemporaries and artists of the following century. Dated around 1575, near the time when Veronese painted the canvases for the ceiling of the Sala del Collegio in the Doge's Palace.

8

7. Jacopo Robusti, known as 'Tintoretto'
(Venice 1519-1594)
and Domenico Robusti, known as 'Tintoretto'
(Venice 1560-1635)

The Dream of Saint Mark

Canvas, 388 × 314 cm
Acquisition: 1924, from the Church of S. Maria degli Angeli at Murano, (cat. 875)
Latest restoration: 1992-93

A collaborative effort by Jacopo Tintoretto and his son Domenico, originally located at the side of the altar in the chapel of the Chapter Room of the Scuola Grande di San Marco, which Jacopo strove to complete in 1585 in order to for his father and two friends to gain acceptance into the Dominican confraternity.

9

10. Paolo Caliari, known as 'Veronese'
(Verona 1528-Venice 1588)

Annunciation

Canvas, 271 × 541 cm
Acquisition: 1812, following the Napoleonic suppressions, (cat. 260)
Latest restoration: 1969-70

From the Scuola dei Mercanti, (still intact and the left of the Church of Madonna dell'Orto), where the piece was kept in the Sala dell'Albergo above the door. The symbol of the confraternity – a hand blessing the cross – can be seen at the centre under the drum, while on the pillars of the middle columns are the coats of arms of the commissioners, the Cadabrazzo and Cottoni families. The work was widely praised by contemporaries. It was painted in 1578, a date revealed by reflection analyses under a thick repainted layer which, together with other alterations (the insertion of a piece of floor on the lower central area near the door, the shortening of the upper part), greatly influence our understanding of the piece. The composition still reveals some excellent details from its original luminosity, such as the vase on the balustrade, and appears as a succession and synthesis of scenic elements, closed at the background by a small temple which was perhaps inspired by the Church of Santa Maria Nuova in Vicenza, completed by Palladio also in 1578.

11. Titian (Tiziano Vecellio)
(Pieve di Cadore c. 1488/90 -Venice 1576)

Pietà

Canvas, 353 × 347 cm
Acquisition: 1814, following the Napoleonic suppressions, (cat. 400)
Latest restoration: 1984-85

This work reached the Accademia from the church of Sant'Angelo, where it had been placed in 1631 at the end of the great plague. Ridolfi in 1648 recalls how it had been created by Titian for the chapel of Cristo at the Frari in exchange for being buried there. But the negotiations failed and the painting, which was created from seven different pieces of canvas, was brought into the workshop. A document recently discovered in the secret Archive of the Vatican confirms that in March of 1575 the painting was displayed at the Frari. In fact, a papal nuncio decree asks that the image, which

10

11

10

12

was placed on an different altar from the one agreed upon, be returned to Titian. In 1576, while the plague was at its worst, Titian had nearly transformed the painting into a large *ex voto* against the epidemic, an exceptional autobiographical statement. As the writing near the bottom attests, the work was definitively completed by Jacopo Palma il Giovane before Titian's death on August 27 of that year: "*Quod Titianus inchoatum reliquit, Palma reventer absolvit deoq dicavit*

opus" ("*that which Titian left unfinished, Palma brought reverently to completion and dedicated the work to God*"). During the most recent restoration project it was revealed how limited Palma's actual intervention was, regarding primarily some touches to camouflage the various grafts of canvas, the angel with the torch painted over a previous putto left unfinished by Titian, and the writing itself. The work is centred largely around the theme of death, eucharistic sacrifice and

resurrection. Like Michelangelo, Titian also portrayed himself in the *Pietà* destined for his grave: the old man lying prostrate in front of the Virgin – probably Nicodemus – is a self-portrait.

12. Paolo Caliari known as 'Veronese'
(Verona 1528–Venice 1588)

Crucifixion

Canvas, 285 cm x 447 cm
Acquisition: 1834, following the Napoleonic suppressions
(cat. 255)

Latest restoration: 1969
The freedom of the *Christ in the House of Levi* is replaced here by a strict adhesion to the evangelical text, a sign of a deep change in the political and religious climate in Venice, surely accelerated by the plague of 1575. The dark and dramatic atmosphere of the scenes are typical of Veronese's last phase, to which the painting belongs; it was completed around 1582 and was originally in the church of San Nicolò della Lattuga at the Frari.

Leandro Bassano, Bernardo Strozzi, Giambattista Tiepolo, Luca Giordano, Jacopo Tintoretto, Bonifacio Veronese and Pordenone

Room 11 was reopened in 1946 by Carlo Scarpa after covering it with a thick grey canvas. This was to be a provisional arrangement while a definitive plan was implemented – which was not to be carried out by Scarpa. In the 1980s, this large room was renovated, repeating the motives used by Scarpa in its twin room (Room 10). In 1996, fragments of the ceiling of the Church of the Scalzi painted by Giambattista Tiepolo were placed here using specially created supports for their display.

Giambattista Tiepolo, The Discovery of the True Cross and Saint Elena, *detail*

1. **Leandro da Ponte, known as 'Bassano'**
(Bassano 1557–1622)

Resurrection of Lazarus

Canvas, 416 × 237 cm
Acquisition: 1815,
following the Napoleonic
suppressions, (cat. 252)
Latest restoration: 1981

Returned from Paris in
1815, this altarpiece was
originally on the high
altar of the Mocenigo
house in the church of
Santa Maria della Carità.
Generally believed to be
from the beginning of
the century, the painting
reveals Bassano's dignified
translation of his father's
artistic language.

Bernardo Strozzi
(Genoa 1581–Venice
1644)

2. *Portrait of the Knight
Giovanni Grimani*

Canvas, 225 × 143 cm
Acquisition: 1981, by
purchase, (cat. 1358)
Latest restoration: 1995

Giovanni Grimani, while
he was ambassador in
Vienna from 1636 to
1640, was knighted by
the Emperor. This large
portrait was probably
ordered from Strozzi
upon his return from
Vienna, immediately after
1640. Grimani is
portrayed with the
golden stole, symbol of
knighthood. This work is
a masterpiece from the
height of Strozzi's artistic
maturity. Hints of
Rubens and Van Dyck are
brought together with a
decidedly Venetian
treatment of light and
colour. The great painters
of the 18th century, from
Fra' Galgario to
Alessandro Longhi and
including Giambattista
Tiepolo himself, will
look to this kind of
portraiture for their
official portraits

1

2

3. *Feast in the House of Simon*

Canvas, 257 × 737 cm
Acquisition: 1911, by
purchase, (cat. 777)
Latest restoration: 1981

This large painting,
purchased in Vicenza in
1911, comes from the
chapel of Palazzo Gorleri
in Genoa. It was probably
originally painted for the
parlour of the Santa
Maria in Passione
monastery in Genoa. In
addition to its attempt to
translate the style of
Caravaggio into a
Baroque setting, the
painting reveals a distinct
Venetian influence, a style
well known to Strozzi
even before he moved to
Venice.

11

3

Giambattista Tiepolo
(Venice, 1696–Madrid 1770)

4. Punishment of the Serpents

Canvas, 167 × 1355 cm
Acquisition: 1892, following
the Napoleonic
suppressions, (cat. 343)
Latest restoration: 1992

This large frieze was
originally under the choir in
the church of Santi Cosma
e Damiano on the
Giudecca. It was owned by
the state after the
Napoleonic suppressions,
and ended up in the church
of Santa Maria e San
Liberale in Castelfranco
Veneto, where it remained

rolled-up for almost sixty
years. These events damaged
the work, but all its
expressive potential remains
intact; indeed, it is precisely
for this reason that the large
gaps have not been filled in.
Dating to around 1731–32,
the painting depicts the
biblical episode of the
bronze serpent erected by
Moses in the desert in order
to heal the snake bites sent
by God to punish the
people of Israel who had
not shown the proper faith
or patience.

5. Moses and Aaron

Fresco, 335 × 446 × 180 cm
(cat. 1376)

*6. Announcement to the Prophet
Nathan*

Fresco, 335 × 446 × 180 cm
(cat. 1378)

7. David and his Wife Mikal

Fresco, 335 × 446 × 180 cm
(cat. 1377)
Latest restoration: 1995-96

The Scalzi Carmelites
commissioned Tiepolo to
decorate the ceiling of the
church of Santa Maria di
Nazareth, the last of the great
religious cycles on fresco by
the artist. The church was

destroyed by an Austrian
bomb intended for the
nearby railway station on the
night of October 24, 1915.
The contract was stipulated
on September 13, 1743 and
on October 1 Girolamo
Mengozzi, nicknamed
Colonna (column), began to
create the artificial
architectural features for the
sum of 1500 ducats; Tiepolo
would receive 3000 ducats
for his work. He studied the
composition in a
considerable number of
sketches and prepared two
oval drafts on canvas: the
first, probably the one for
which he was paid 100

5

zecchini on September 13, 1743, is preserved in the Accademia Gallery (Room 17, cat. 91); the second, which was closest to the final version, is today at the Paul Getty Museum in Malibu. Both painters received payments from April 14 until November 23, 1745, dates which should also correspond to the actual execution of the vast work. On the central part was celebrated the miraculous *Transportation of the Holy House of Nazareth*. In the decoration on the perimeter of the vault were other episodes depicting

various parts of the Old Testament foreshadowing Mary herself, or the theme and the Holy House. Another four pendentives, one of which is lost, depicted annunciation scenes. Recovered from the depository where they had been stored after the disaster, they were then transferred onto canvas in 1969. The last part of the work restored the slightly curved shape. On the first, a few condensed episodes from Exodus are represented: Moses, angered by the smelting of the golden calf, breaks the tablets of the law

bestowed upon him by God, which will be given to him a second time. Returning from Mount Sinai, his face becomes radiant after having spoken with the Lord and thus he appears to Aaron. On the second, God, in the form of an angel, announces to the prophet Nathan his alliance with David and the permanence of his dynasty, the depository of the messianic promises. On the last one, David responds harshly to his wife Mikal, who had chastised him for humiliating himself by dancing before the ark of

the Lord. The extraordinary power of the line, the suggestion of the green tones on the light background and the effective synthesis make these fragments – which are clearly by the artist himself, at least the figurative parts – works of the utmost quality. As documentation also confirms, the backgrounds belong to Mengozzi, while Tiepolo had to unify the whole work with small retouches. His unmistakable luminous brushstrokes are found in many areas on these three pendentives and on the following four loggias.

11

6

7

8

9

10

11

12

Giambattista Tiepolo
(Venice, 1696–Madrid
1770)

8. *Worshipers Facing
a Loggia*

Detached fresco,
405 × 216 cm (cat. 836)

9. *Loggia*

Detached fresco,
405 × 216 cm (cat. 1375)

10. *Worshipers Facing
a Loggia*

Detached fresco,
405 × 216 cm (cat. 837)

11. *Worshipers Facing
a Loggia*

Detached fresco,
405 × 216 cm (cat. 1374)
Latest restoration:
1995/96

At the four curved
corners of the ceiling
were some railed galleries
which survived the
bombing and were
recovered between 1916
and 1917. Two of these
(cat. 836 and 837) were
displayed at the
Accademia Galleries in
1919, the other two
remained in storage until
the most recent
restoration. On three
of these, Tiepolo painted
some praying worshipers,
awed spectators
of the miracle.
The fourth, which is
empty, should belong
to Colonna, but here
as in the other loggias,
Tiepolo surely intervened

with some corrections in
order to render the work
more uniform.

12. *Saint Helena and the
Discovery of the True Cross*

Canvas, diam. 500 cm
Acquisition: 1812
(cat. 462)
Latest restoration: 1982

The large ceiling painting
was made for the church
of Le Cappuccine in
Castello, which was
destroyed. The painting
was surrounded by
decorations by Girolamo
Mengozzi (Colonna).
From about the same
time as the first works
delivered in 1743 by
Tiepolo to the Scuola
dei Carmini, it shares

with these the marvellous
chromatic polyphony and
refined 'upside-down'
perspective. A sketch
showing an early idea
for the painting is also
on display here
(cat. 789, Room 17).

13. **Luca Giordano**
(Naples 1634–1705)

Crucifixion of Saint Peter

Canvas, 195 × 257 cm
Acquisition: 1910, by
purchase, (cat. 751)
Latest restoration: 1984

The signature and the
date are on the painting:
"L. Giordano F. 1692",
but these have been
recognised as false. The
authorship is certain, but
the date is less so, with
critics generally placing
the work – still with
some exceptions –
around 1659-60. The
dramatic component of
the composition evokes
the paintings of
Caravaggio, but the
dilution of the forms into
the colours prefigures a
Rococo style.

13

11

14

**Jacopo Robusti
known as 'Tintoretto'**
(Venice 1519-1594)

14. Madonna dei Camerlenghi

Canvas, 221 × 520cm
Acquisition: 1883, (cat. 210)
Latest restoration: 1992

This large painting, also
known as the *Madonna of
the Treasurers*, carries an
inscription on the lower
left: "unanimis concordiae/
simbolus/1566". The work
was destined for the
Camerlenghi palazzo at
Rialto. The Camerlenghi
were the financial
magistrates of the Venetian
Republic. The date of 1566
refers to the offices of
Michele Pisani, Lorenzo
Dolfin and Marino
Malipiero, whose coats of
arms are shown on the
plinth to the lower left, but
the actual execution of the
piece occurred when
Marino Malipiero's
command ended in around
1567, a date which can
actually be seen under
magnification just below

that of 1566. The
horizontal development of
the composition,
emphasised by the
succession of porticoes
with the marvellous
landscape beyond them,
and the penetrating
characterisation of the
commissioners followed by
their secretaries make this
work masterpiece of the
Venetian votive painting
tradition.

15. Crucifixion

Canvas, 280 × 444 cm
Acquisition: 1891, from the
Scuola del Rosario in the
church of Santi Giovanni e
Paolo, (cat. 213)
Latest restoration: 1967

Originally in the Scuola
del Santissimo
Sacramento, in the
Venetian church of San
Severo, this piece dates to
around 1554-55 and
reveals a period in which
Tintoretto embraced the
painting of Paolo
Veronese.

11

16. Bonifacio de' Pitati known as 'Bonifacio Veronese'
(Verona 1487–Venice 1553)

Lazarus the Beggar

Canvas, 206 × 438 cm
Acquisition: 1812, by purchase, (cat. 291)
Latest restoration: 1991-92

Purchased from the Grimani family for the Accademia Galleries at the request for the viceroy Eugenio Beauharnais; originally the piece was in the Giustiniani palazzo, where it was still recorded in 1763. Dated around 1543-45, this is considered the artist's masterpiece for his ability to bring together the teachings of both Titian and Tintoretto. The episode depicted here refers to the evangelical parable of Epulone refusing to give alms to poor Lazarus, but here this becomes the pretext for an extraordinary description of Venetian villa life.

17. Giovanni Antonio de' Sacchis, known as 'Pordenone'
(Pordenone 1483/84–Ferrara 1539)

The Blessed Lorenzo Giustiniani and Saints

Canvas, 420 × 222 cm
Acquisition: 1815, following the Napoleonic suppressions, (cat. 316)
Latest restoration: 1997

This altarpiece was commissioned from Pordenone in 1532 for 100 ducats, and was for the altar of the Renier family, which is still in the Church of Madonna dell'Orto. Brought to Paris in 1797, it was returned to Venice in 1815 and entrusted to the Accademia Galleries. The figure of Lorenzo Giustiniani – canonised in 1690 – blesses Saints Louis, Francis, Bernard, John the Baptist and two "turchini", who were secular canons from San Giorgio in Alga, to which order the church was entrusted. The articulation of the composition, the elongated modes and twists of the figures, and in particular the pose of the Michelangelesque body of John the Baptist, are all characteristics of mannerism, which was effectively introduced in Veneto by Pordenone himself.

11

16

11

17

Marco Ricci, Giuseppe Zais
and Francesco Zuccarelli

This room is formed by the long end of the Palladio hallway, with its large windows – probably the work of Lazzari in the 19th century. In 1912 three doors and their awnings were installed; these may have come from a palazzo in Brescia, and were painted by Pietro Scalvini (Brescia, 1718-1792) and Saverio Gandini (Cremona, c. 1729-Brescia, 1796). On the door with the depiction of a sculpture is the Scalvini's signature and the date of 1778.

Francesco Zuccarelli,
The Abduction
of Europe, *detail*

1

2

Marco Ricci
(Belluno 1676-Venice 1730)

1. *Landscape with a Stream, Monks and Washerwomen*

Canvas, 136 × 98 cm
Acquisition: 1878, by purchase, (cat. 457)
Latest restoration: 1963

2. *Landscape with Horses at the Trough*

Canvas, 136 × 198 cm
Acquisition: 1878, by purchase, (cat. 456)
Latest restoration: 1963

These two *pendants* are recorded in the Cormani Algarotti gallery in Treviso.
In the first the Piave valley is discernable, and it also seems to appear in the second, where an old fountain is also shown. With its vivid and attentive realism, the piece is of fundamental importance amongst the output the artist, who was inspired by the drawings of Titian and the engravings of Domenico Campagnola. Originally the piece was thought to be from 1720, but more recently critics have correctly dated in towards 1715.

Giuseppe Zais, attr.
(Canale d'Agordo 1709 -Treviso 1781)

3. *Landscape with Agar and the Angel*

Canvas, 71 × 94 cm

4. *Landscape with Tobias and the Angel*

Canvas, 72 cm × 96 cm
Acquisition: 1906, by purchase, (cat. 721, 722)
Latest restoration: 1984

These two paintings, with the two biblical stories immersed in the landscape – as they also occur in Fetti's *Parables* – are traditionally attributed to Zais, although they seem closer to the style of Antonio Diziani.

3

4

12

5

6

Giuseppe Zais
(Canale d'Agordo 1709
-Treviso 1781)

5. *Ancient Ruins with a
Large Arch and Columns*

Canvas, 96 × 146 cm
Acquisition: 1923, from
the Palazzo Reale, (cat.
847)
Latest restoration: 1984

6. *Landscape with a Stream
and Dancing Villagers*

Canvas, 96 × 142 cm
Acquisition: 1923, from
the Palazzo Reale (Royal
Palace, (cat. 848)
Latest restoration: 1984

In these landscapes from
the end of the 1730s, the
influence of Marco Ricci
on Zais's work is quite
clear; Zais renders Ricci's
style more elegant, but
keeps it vivid and bright.

7. **Francesco Zuccarelli**
(Pitigliano 1702-Florence
1788/89)

Rape of Europa

Canvas, 143 × 208 cm
Acquisition: 1923, from
the Palazzo Reale,
(cat. 858)
Latest restoration: 1982

On the collar of the dog
at the lower left is the
signature. This canvas, like
its *pendant* with the
Bacchanal (Room 12, cat.
859), was painted for the
Pisani family, who kept it
in their splendid and
regal villa in Stra. It is
considered the artist's
masterpiece, and dates to
around 1740-1750. The
story of the rape of
Europa, taken from
Ovid's *Metamorphoses*, is
rendered with the same
grace and ease as an
Metastasian melodrama.

12

7

Giuseppe Zais
(Canale d'Agordo 1709–
Treviso 1781)

8. *Landscape with a River,
Bridge and Flocks*

Canvas, 97 × 142 cm
Acquisition: 1923, from the
Palazzo Reale, (cat. 849)
Latest restoration: 1985

9. *Ruins of a Vaulted Building*

Canvas, 97 × 147 cm
Acquisition: 1923, from the
Palazzo Reale (cat. 846)
Latest restoration: 1984

Marco Ricci's influence on
Zais is also evident in these
paintings from the end of
the 1730s. Zais renders
Ricci's style more elegant,
but keeps it vivid and bright.

Francesco Zuccarelli
(Pitigliano, 1702–Florence,
1788/89)

10. *Landscape with a Lady on
Horseback*

Canvas, transported from
another canvas, 115 × 133 cm
Acquisition: 1923, from the
Palazzo Reale (cat. 861)
Latest restoration: 1984

11. *Landscape with a Boy
Fishing*

Canvas, 116 × 135 cm
Acquisition: 1923, from the
Palazzo Reale (cat. 862)
Latest restoration: 1985

These two landscapes once
belonged to the Pisani
family, and date to around
1740-50. They present with
gentle and festive grace and
fresh colours the pastoral
theme that was so dear to
18th century poetics.

8

9

12

10

11

Giuseppe Zais
(Canale d'Agordo 1709 –
Treviso 1781)

12. *Bacchanal*

Canvas, 142 × 209 cm
Acquisition: 1923,
from the Palazzo Reale
(cat. 859)
Latest restoration: 1982

Pendant of the *Abduction
of Europe* (cat. 858, Room
12), also belonging to the
Pisani family and painted
during the same period.
While fauns and nymphs
dance together in the
idyllic landscape, the
drunk Bacchus rests in
the shade of a rustic hut.

13. *Hunt for the Bull*

Canvas, 114 × 150 cm
Acquisition: 1949, from
the Palazzo Reale
(cat. 864)
Latest restoration: 1984

Originally in the
Benedictine convent of
San Giorgio Maggiore,
this work is considered to
be from the early period
of the artist's career, a
little after 1732, when he
arrived in Venice. Even
the bloody episode here

of the hunt for the bull
is interpreted with a
pastoral grace, and the
work was widely praised
in artistic centres such as
Paris and London, where
the artist sojourned.

13

14

14. **Antonio Diziani**
(Venice 1737-1797)

Landscape with Mary Magdalene

Canvas, 132 × 117 cm
Acquisition: 1807, from the old Accademia, (cat. 455)

This is the painting that Antonio Diziani – the son of the more famous Gaspare – presented in 1766 to gain admittance to the Accademia, into which he was accepted only on 11th September, 1774.

Gaspare Diziani
(Belluno 1689-Venice 1767)

15. *Moses and the Burning Bush*

Canvas, 56 × 96 cm

16. *Moses and the Tablets of the Law*

Canvas, 56 × 96 cm
Acquisition: 1838, following the Napoleonic suppressions, (cat. 459, 460)
Latest restoration: 1980

These two *pendants* are largely considered to have been painted in collaboration with the artist's son Antonio, who worked on the landscape.

15

17. Francesco Zuccarelli
(Pitigliano 1702–Florence 1788–89)

Landscape with a Resting Hunter

Canvas, 79 × 97 cm
Acquisition: 1959, from
the Palazzo Reale,
(cat. 1333)
Latest restoration: 1993

Originally perhaps in the convent of San Giorgio Maggiore, this painting – of which there is a copy on the antiquities market – dates to around the 1740s. The typical idyllic representation of nature is strong in the group with the resting hunter, the horse and the two dogs, rendered with an unusual naturalness. This aspect reveals Zuccarelli's familiarity with Dutch landscape artists such as Berchem and Wouwermann.

17

12

16

Jacopo Bassano and portraits by Jacopo Tintoretto

Obtained by the unification of three cells of the Carità convent with the first remodelling projects, the ceiling of the first area, which had previously been under a large canvas, was recovered, revealing the decoration by Tranquillo Orsi. The remodelling was performed by Carlo Scarpa in 1947.

Jacopo Bassano,
Adoration of the
Shepherds, *detail*

13.

1

13

3

1. Jacopo da Ponte, known as 'Bassano', and his workshop
(Bassano 1517-1592)

Landscape with Shepherd and the Burning Bush

Canvas, 45 × 114 cm
Acquisition: 1838, donation from Girolamo Contarini, (cat. 415)
Latest restoration: 1963

Originally attributed to Jacopo, today it is believed to have come from his workshop, perhaps derived from models by Francesco Bassano.

Jacopo da Ponte, known as 'Bassano'
(Bassano 1517-1592)

2. Adoration of the Shepherds

Canvas, 95 × 140cm
Acquisition: 1983, by purchase, (cat. 1360)

This may be the painting identified in 1620 in the Giusti del Giardino collection, indeed, the piece was purchased from Count Justo Giusti himself. Nonetheless, Ridolfi also makes

mention in 1648 of the existence of a very similar work in the house of Cristoforo Orsetti, in which Bassano was believed to imitate "the elegance of Padovanino". In this composition, which evokes Titian-like themes, there is a unique blend of Parmigianino influences (most evident in the image of the Virgin), mannerist refinement and naturalistic observations in the depiction of the animals and the faces of the shepherds. It dates to 1545 or shortly after.

3. Rest in Egypt

Canvas, 52 × 102 cm
Acquisition: 1838, donation from Girolamo Contarini, (cat. 410)

The main group of the Madonna with the two children is found in other works by Bassano. The painting recalls a composition described by Ridolfi (1648) in the house of the artist's great-grandson at Bassano.

13

2

13

4

Jacopo Robusti, known as 'Tintoretto'
(Venice 1519-1594)

4. *Portrait of the Procurator Antonio Cappello*

Canvas, 114 × 80 cm
Acquisition: 1812, following the Napoleonic suppressions, (cat. 236)
Latest restoration: 1993-94

The identification of the portrait rests on a now lost 19th century document. The portrait is of Antonio Cappello, from the San Polo area of Venice and born probably in 1494.
He carried out many demanding tasks – including that of Procurator in 1525 – for the Republic until his death in 1565. The portrait is from the Procuratia de' Supra (the office in Saint Mark's Square of the procurators concerned primarily with the Basilica and its treasures), where sources record its presence, even attributing it to Titian. The *ante quem* date for the piece is 1565, when Cappello died. Indeed, the work is similar to other official portraits painted in the early 1560s which also bear the mark of Titian's influence.

5. *Portrait of Battista Morosini*

Canvas, 96 × 57 cm
Acquisition: 1838, by donation from Girolamo Contarini, (cat. 237)
Latest restoration: 1993-94

The identification of the subject is based on the Tintoretto-inspired portrait in the Doge's Palace, where Battista Morosini appears older, and by this time is Procurator. The son of Francesco, Battista was born in 1537 and died in 1598. The painting appears to be the product of polished routine, but also reveals a studied effort from the artist. It dates to before 1573.

6. Andrea Michieli, known as 'Vicentino'
(Vicenza 1542-1617)

Paradise

Canvas, 116 × 86 cm
Acquisition: 1978, by purchase, (cat. 1354)

This is the first preparatory study for the *Paradise* in the Basilica dei Frari, and dates to the beginning of the 17th century. Another study can be found in the Walker Art Gallery in Liverpool. The influence of Tintoretto – the 16th century artist most imitated by Venetian late-mannerists, of whom Vicentino is a good example – in this composition is quite evident.

13

5

6

7. Jacopo Negretti, known as 'Palma il Giovane'
(Venice 1548-1628)

The Crucifixion of Saint Peter

Canvas, 168 × 132 cm
Acquisition: 1901, donation from M. Guggenheim, (cat. 660)
Latest restoration: 1963

Probably an early idea for a ceiling work, which is today unknown or perhaps was never constructed. On the upper part, with the Trinity and the Virgin at the centre surrounded by angels and the symbols of the Passion, and on the lower portion with the blessed, including Adam and Eve, the artist imitates a signed composition which is in a private collection in Rome. The crucifixion scene seems to betray a continuing influence of the Michelangelo fresco in the Paolina Chapel. The work dates to about 1614.

8. Domenico Robusti, known as 'Tintoretto'
(Venice 1560-1635)

Portrait of a Contarini Procurator

Canvas, 117 × 87 cm
Acquisition: 1919, following the Napoleonic suppressions, (cat. 1012)
Latest restoration: 1993

The painting was originally in the Procuratia de Citra (the office in Saint Mark's Square for the Procurators of the Basilica who dealt with its holdings on 'this side' – 'de Citra' – of the Grand Canal), and carries the Contarini coat of arms and the initials L.C. at the lower left. The work is probably a portrait of Giovanni Paolo Contarini, who was elected Procurator in 1594 and died in 1604.

9. Jacopo da Ponte, known as 'Bassano'
(Bassano 1517-1592)

Saint Eleutherius Blesses the Devotees

Canvas, 280 × 174 cm
Acquisition: 1829, following the Napoleonic suppressions (cat. 401)
Latest restoration: 1993

Originally on the high altar of the church of Sant'Eleuterio in Vicenza, belonging to the Marzari confraternity. Recently critics have dated the work at 1565. It is probably a collaboration with the artist's son Francesco – perhaps a depiction of the young man in prayer – which must have begun even at the planning stage, and is especially evident in the weak Christ amongst the clouds.

8

7

13

9

13

12

10. Jacopo Robusti known as 'Tintoretto'
(Venice 1519-1594)

The Procurator Andrea Cappello

Canvas, 115 × 86 cm
Acquisition: 1812,
following the Napoleonic
suppressions, (cat. 234)
Latest restoration: 1994

Originally in the
Procuratia de Supra, this
piece is probably the one
indicated in 1812 by
Pietro Edwards (the first
curator of the Accademia
Galleries) as the *Portrait of
a Veneto Senator* by Jacopo
Tintoretto. On the right
are the Cappello coat of

arms and the initial "A".
The subject is indeed
Andrea Cappello, son of
Silvano, who was elected
procurator in 1537 and
died in 1564, the *ante
quem* date for the
completion of the portrait,
which was obviously
painted from life.

11. Jacopo da Ponte known as Bassano
(Bassano 1517-1592)

Saint Jerome

Canvas, 119 × 154 cm
Acquisition: 1900, by
purchase, (cat. 652)

Dating to the beginning
of the 1560s, this is

almost certainly the same painting seen by Ridolfi (1648) in the Widmann house. It is unanimously recognised as one of the artist's masterpieces, revealing a great sense of monumentality. The artist has one eye on the German figurative tradition and the other on the harmony between hermit and nature, a characteristic of Giovanni Bellini. He also adds a decidedly modern psychological aspect: the reluctance of Jerome to continue striking himself. Indeed, the saint holds the stone stained with blood almost hidden behind his back while he ponders the sacrifice of the cross. He is surrounded by the usual attributes, which are fine still-lifes in their own right.

12. **Titian (Tiziano Vecellio)**
(Pieve di Cadore c. 1480-90-Venice 1576)
Virgin with Child

Canvas, 124 × 96 cm
Acquisition: 1981, bequest from the will of Leonardo Albertini, (cat. 1359)

For private devotion, this painting belonged to the Matenza Marquises of Milan, at least from 1616 until 1879, when it passed to the Pinetti Martinengo family of Bergamo. It was purchased in 1916 by Luigi Albertini, father of Leonardo. To the left of the composition can be seen the burning bush, symbol of the eternal virginity of Mary. X-rays have revealed that the artist used a canvas for this painting on which he had previously painted a praying saint. From about 1560.

10

13

11

13

Jacopo Robusti, known as 'Tintoretto'
(Venice 1519-1594)

13. *Salomon and the Queen of Saba*

Canvas, 122 × 127 cm
Acquisition: 1988, with the recoveries by Rodolfo Sivieri, (cat. 1381)

This painting was originally in a private collection in Bologna, then in the Simotti Rocchi collection in Rome; it was finally recovered in Germany in 1954 by Rodolfo Siviero. The painting is part of a series of allegorical subjects taken from episodes the Old and New Testaments, which have been attributed to Tintoretto's early phase, when he was closest to Andrea Schiavone, around 1545.

14. *The Procurator Jacopo Soranzo*

Canvas, 106 × 90 cm
Acquisition: 1812, following the Napoleonic suppressions, (cat. 245)
Latest restoration: 1957

Painted for the Procuratoria de Supra, this work was originally in the form of a lunette, and to make it rectangular it was joined at the top – on the left with a triangular piece of canvas and on the right with a short strip to frame Soranzo. The alteration probably took place at the end of the 1500s, when many paintings were adapted by Tintoretto and his son Domenico for the new rooms of the rebuilt Procurators' Offices. The fragmentary writing carries the name of the subject and the date of 1522, which indicates when Soranzo took office and not when the painting was completed. The portrait dates to around 1550, just after the portrait of Soranzo with a group of relatives, today at the Castello Sforzesco in Milan. Both paintings are from before 1551, however, the year the Procurator died. Despite its official "formal" use, the picture reveals a surprising expressive power.

14

16

15. *Portrait of Doge Alvise Mocenigo*

Canvas, 116 × 97 cm
Acquisition: 1817, following the Napoleonic suppressions, (cat. 233)
Latest restoration: 1993

From the Procuratoria de Ultra, the office in Saint Mark's Square of the Procurators who dealt with the Basilica's holdings on the other side – Ultra – of the Grand Canal. As with the preceding portrait, this one was originally in the form of a lunette, and depicts Alvise Mocenigo, who was born in 1507 and served as Doge from 1570 until 1577, the year the portrait was made, probably just after the election. In the noble pose and sober tonality can be seen the influence of the style of portraiture practised by Titian, whom Tintoretto had succeeded as the official portrait artist of the Signoria.

16. **Veneto School of the 16ᵗʰ Century**

Allegory of Nature

Panel, 42 × 74 cm
Acquisition: during the 19ᵗʰ century, from the Palazzo Reale (cat. 901)
Latest restoration: 1960

This panel, which shows the *Allegory of Nature*

15

between *Time* and *Truth*, is recorded as having been in the Zecca (mint) in 1788, and passed to Palazzo Reale at the beginning of the 19ᵗʰ century. Previously it was attributed to Andrea Meldolla, known as 'Schiavone' (Zadar, 1522–Venice, 1563), but later it was thought to be from the studio of Bonifacio de' Pitati, known as 'Bonifacio Veronese' (Verona, 1487-Venice, 1553).

17. **Lambert Sustris**
(Amsterdam, around 1515-Venice, after 1591?)

Christ Bound, and a View of Jerusalem

Panel, 63 × 80 cm
Acquisition: 1816, bequest from Girolamo Molin, (cat. 268)
Latest restoration: 1959

The painting came to the Galleries when it was attributed to Schiavone, but the panel is now recognised as the work of Sutris, who often painted scenes of Jerusalem taken from models by the Sutris' first master, Jan van Scorel.

17

13

17th-century paintings.
Currently closed for restoration

This room has undergone the same renovations as Room 13.
The paintings currently on display cannot be visited.

Domenico Fetti, David
with Goliath's head,
detail

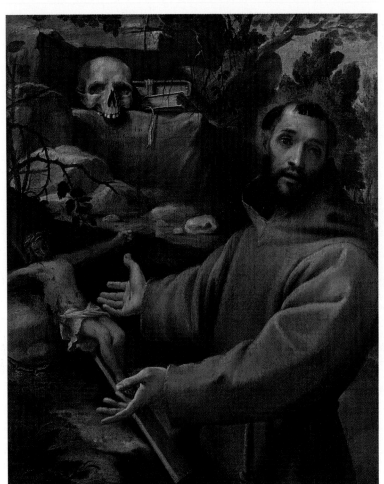

3. Pierfrancesco Mola
(Coldrerio 1612-1666)

Allegory of the Phlegmatic Temperament

Canvas, 76 × 114 cm
Acquisition: 1955, by
purchase, (cat. 1314)
Latest restoration: 1962

This painting was
inspired by Carlo Ripa's
Iconologia (Padua, 1630),
in which the relationship
between the four
elements and human
temperament is
established: "the choleric
for fire", "the sanguine
for air", "the melancholy
for earth", and "the
phlegmatic for water".
The figure of the
sleeping man represents
the "phlegmatic/water"
element. As the fountain
indicates, the early study
of Guercino's work is
enriched by exposure to
Veneto artistic culture.
The work dates to
around the middle of the
century.

1. Annibale Carracci
(Bologna 1560-1609)

Saint Francis

Canvas, 91 × 73 cm
Acquisition: 1901, by
purchase, (cat. 1189)
Latest restoration: 1955

An early work from
around 1585-1586, this
painting – of which there
are copies in the Galleria
Nazionale in Rome and
in the Liechtenstein
collection in Vaduz –
reflects in its great
elegance the influence of
the major Veneto painters
of the 1500s. The
landscape is marvellous,
with its symbolic
elements which are
equally valid as still lifes
in their own right.

2. Bernardo Strozzi
(Genova 1581/82
-Venice 1644)

San Jerome

Canvas, 56 × 47 cm
Acquisition: 1838, by
donation from Girolamo
Contarini, (cat. 424)
Latest restoration: 1962

This devotional painting
of a theme repeated
many times by the artist
is generally attributed to
the early period of
Strozzi's stay in Venice,
around the 1640s.

14

3

4. **Domenico Fetti**
(Rome? 1588/89 –
Venice 1623)

*Parable of the Good
Samaritan*

Panel, 61 × 45 cm
Acquisition: 1838, by
donation from Girolamo
Contarini (cat. 503)
Latest restoration: 1948

"Parables" are among the
most common subjects
treated by Fetti, such as
this one of the good
Samaritan. Like its
preparatory drawing at the
Louvre (inv. 3069), this
work dates to about 1617.
There are various replicas
of the subject, including
the Gemäldegalerie one
in Dresden, which depicts
the subject in a horizontal
format.

14

4

5. **Johann Liss**
(Holstein c. 1597–Verona 1631)

Apollo and Marsyas

Canvas, 58 × 48 cm
Acquisition: 1838, by donation from Girolamo Contarini, (cat. 674)

Among the last works by the painter, incorporating his experience in Venice with his earlier training in Rome from the Dutch admirers of Caravaggio.

6. **Domenico Fetti** copy from (Rome? 1588/89–Venezia 1623)

Portrait of Francesco Andreini

Canvas, 102 × 79 cm
Acquisition: 1838, donation from Girolamo Contarini, (cat. 678)
Latest restoration: 1956

A copy of the portrait of the actor Francesco Andreini (Pistoia, c. 1548-Mantua, 1624) kept at the Hermitage in Saint Petersburg. This painting mimics 16th century Venetian or Carpaccio-inspired models, and dates to before 1620, when Andreini left Mantua and headed first for Milan, then to France, returning only after the sudden departure of Fetti. The painting depicts the subject with a mask in his hand, symbol of his profession, and uniquely recalls Eduardo De Filippo, thereby obtaining further depth, depicting not only Francesco Andreini but every actor, beyond every limit of time.

Johann Liss
(Holstein c. 1597–Verona 1631)

7. *The Sacrifice of Isaac*

Canvas, 66 × 85 cm
Acquisition: 1932, by purchase, (cat. 914)
Latest restoration: 1959

8. *Abel Mourned by his Parents*

Canvas, 68 × 89 cm
Acquisition: 1932, by purchase, (cat. 913)
Latest restoration: 1959

This painting, along with the previous one of which it is a *pendant*, was purchased from the Giovanelli collection. Both paintings date to the years when the artist sojourned in Venice (1624-29). The dramatic effect of the subject is diluted in a powerful melancholy, a result of the emphasis given to the landscape where the event is taking place. *The Sacrifice* is one of Liss' masterpieces; there are other versions of the second painting, with variations.

5

6

7

14

8

131

9

10

11

9. Tiberio Tinelli
(Venice 1586-1638)

Portrait of Luigi Molin

Canvas, 133 × 115 cm
Acquisition: 1816,
bequest from Girolamo
Molin, (cat. 544)
Latest restoration: 1962

The attribution to Tinelli
– like the identification
of the subject – have by
now been widely
accepted. According to
Ridolfi (1648), Molin
was sent to Mantua by
the Venetian Republic in
1637 for the election of
the new Duke, Carlo II,
and brought Tinelli with
him. The gentleman rests
on a book which, with its
Ducal seal, could well be
the "Commissione
Ducale", containing
instructions for running
the Republic. The busts
in the background in this
case could allude to his
passion for collecting art.

**10. Anonymous,
17ᵗʰ Century**

*Portrait of Procurator
Domenico Contarini*

Canvas, 163 × 102 cm
Acquisition: 1988, with
the recoveries by Rodolfo
Sivieri, (cat. 1382)
Latest restoration: 1988

Recorded in 1927 in the
Giovanelli collection at
San Felice, the piece was
taken by the Nazis and
recovered by Rodolfo
Siviero. It has been
attributed to Nicolas
Regnier, from a time
when his style was
particularly similar to that
of his son-in-law Daniel
van der Dyck. Tiberio
Tinelli has also been
mentioned but after
careful scrutiny of the
best Venetian official
portraits by artists from
Bombelli to Strozzi, the
work's author remains
difficult to identify, in
spite of its obvious
quality.

11. Bernardo Strozzi
(Genova 1581/82
-Venice 1644)

Doge Francesco Erizzo

Canvas, 133 × 108 cm
Acquisition: 1920,
by purchase, (cat. 829)
Latest restoration: 1995

The portrait of Francesco
Erizzo – "Del Prete
Genovese" ("By the
Genovese Priest"),
as is stated in two old
inscriptions on the back
of the original canvas –
was originally in the
Erizzo family villa in
Bassano. The family
commissioned the work
from Strozzi, and it was
to be for private
enjoyment; a replica –
which was the official
portrait in the Doge's
Palace – exists in the
Kunsthistorisches
Museum in Vienna.
Erizzo became Doge in
1631 at the age of 65,
and held the title until his
death in 1646. It is
probable, then, given the
apparent age of the
subject, that the portrait
was made immediately
after his election. It is
probably one of the first
portraits painted in
Venice. Reflectographic

analyses have revealed a
conspicuous correction
on the right hand, and
also confirmed the actual
authorship.

12. Mattia Preti
(Taverna 1613-1699)

Homer

Canvas, 102 × 81 cm
Acquisition: 1821,
by purchase, (cat. 59)
Latest restoration: 1963

When this piece came to
the Accademia it was
believed to be a work by
Caravaggio; later it was
attributed to
Pierfrancesco Mola, but
today it is unanimously
attributed to the early
years of Mattia Preti.

13. Anonymous, 17th Century

A Girl Reading

Canvas, 74 × 69 cm
Acquisition: 1838,
donation from Girolamo
Contarini, (cat. 518)
Latest restoration: 1961

Originally attributed to
Domenico Fetti, the
piece is notable for the
naturalness of the girl
absorbed in her reading.

14. An imitator of Giambattista Langetti
(Genova 1625-Venezia
1676)

Isaac and Jacob

Canvas, 101 × 75 cm
Acquisition: 1838,
donation from Girolamo
Contarini, (cat. 675)

Previously considered to

be the work of
Domenico Fetti; it has
now been correctly
attributed to Langetti's
circle.

12

14

13

14

Domenico Fetti
(Rome? 1588/89–Venice 1623)

15. *David*

Canvas, 175 × 128 cm
Acquisition: 1838, donation from Girolamo Contarini, (cat. 669)
Latest restoration: 1996

The painting came to the Galleries from a descendent of Giorgio Contarini dagli Scrigni, a patron of Fetti in Venice. It dates from between 1617 and 1619, prior to when the artist resided in Venice. The young man, with his indolent beauty and contemporary dress, harks to Caravaggio's elegant knights in *Buona Ventura* (Lucky Fate) or *The Martyrdom of Saint Matthew*. The face bears some similarity to the one used for the *David* in Dresden (Gemäldegalerie) and in Moscow (Pushkin Museum).

16. *Meditation*

Canvas, 179 × 140cm
Acquisition: 1838, donation from Girolamo Contarini, (cat. 671)
Latest restoration: 1961

Although the donator was a descendent of Giorgio Contarini dagli Scrigni, a

15

patron of Fetti in Venice, this famous painting is believed to have been completed around 1618, before the artist actually resided in Venice. The good fortune of the piece is evidenced by the numerous copies and replicas. There were also some illustrious antecedents such as Dürer's famous engraving, *Melancholy* (1514), or the *Vision of Saint Helena* by Paolo Veronese, or the *Magdalene* by Correggio. In spite of the traditional title, it is likely that the artist kept in mind a part of the second Letter of Paul in the Corinthians 2 (7, 10), which holds that Christian "sadness" that produces repentance leads to salvation, while worldly "sadness" brings on death. The female figure is situated between the still life of the lower part of the painting alluding to death and the "sadness of the world". The grapevine above symbolises life and salvation.

16

education in Tuscany, offers here a free and imaginative interpretation of the subject at the end of the 1640s.

Francesco Maffei
(Vicenza, c. 1605–Padua, 1660)

18. *Mythological Scene*

Canvas, 130 × 160 cm
Acquisition: 1968 by purchase, (cat. 1341)
Latest restoration: 1968

19. *Perseus Beheading Medusa*

Canvas, 130 × 160 cm
Acquisition: 1968 by purchase, (cat. 1340)
Latest restoration: 1968

These two *pendants*, one inspired by Ovid's *Metamorphoses* and the other depicting perhaps Circes and Ulysses, were kept in Budapest until the beginning of this century and ended up in an American collection. They date to 1660, and show the free and whimsical imagination of Maffei, who was raised on the innovative pictorial work of Fetti, Liss and Strozzi.

17

17. **Sebastiano Mazzoni**
(Florence? 1611-Venice 1678)

The Annunciation

Canvas, 154 × 112 cm
Acquisition: 1945, from the domanial church of Santa Caterina, (cat. 329)
Latest restoration: 1956

Documented in the church of Santa Caterina, Venice, at the beginning of the nineteenth century, the painting should perhaps be identified with the *Annunciation*, documented in the church of San Luca dal Boschini in 1664. Mazzoni, who had received his early artistic

18

20. Pietro Muttoni, known as 'della Vecchia'
(Venice, 1603-Venice, 1678)

Votive Painting

Canvas, 285 × 227 cm
Acquisition: beginning of the 19th century, following the Napoleonic suppressions, (cat. 868)
Latest restoration: 1961

At the lower centre the words "ex voto" and at the right the initials of the author and the date 1640. The work alludes perhaps to a religious conversion. In the sky to the left appears Saint Giustina, whose church originally housed the work; in the foreground is a lady adorned with jewels, seated at the top of some stairs. An angel shows her a skull, a symbol of the transience of life; at the sides are Saint Joseph and Saint John the Evangelist. The vibrancy of the palette and the unique invention are characteristics of Muttoni's work. He was called 'della Vecchia' for his ability to restore and imitate the 'old' Venetian masters, Giorgione and Titian in particular.

20

21

21. Giulio Carpioni
(Venezia? 1613-Vicenza 1679)

Crucifixion

Canvas, 205 × 131 cm
Acquisition: 1967, following the Napoleonic suppressions, (cat. 1339)
Latest restoration: 1968

This work was originally in the Church of Santa Lucia in Udine, and may belong to the first period of the artist's stay in Vicenza. Carpioni reacted against the late-mannerism conformity by painting very rigorous forms, presenting accents of plasticism and naturalism as in some of the figures at the foot of the cross.

19

14

Giovanni Antonio Pellegrini, Giambattista Tiepolo and Giannantonio Guardi

This is the final part of the long Palladio corridor. The "cell" structure (Rooms 16 and 16a) is to the left, while within the building itself is a large exhibition space that was created from joining three rooms (into Room 17); a door remains from one of these rooms. Towards the rear, through the large doorway is found the famous oval stairway designed by Palladio in 1561.

Giannantonio Guardi, Herminia and Vaprinus Happen upon the Wounded Tancredi, *detail*

1

4

2

3

15

1. **Giambattista Tiepolo**
(Venice, 1696–Madrid, 1770)

Apparition of the Sacred Family to Saint Gaetanus

Canvas, 128 × 73 cm
Acquisition: 1887, by purchase, (cat. 481)
Latest restoration: 1970

Originally painted for the altar of the small chapel of Palazzo Labia in Venice. The sacred image here is conceived in a new way, outside a classical building.
Dates to 1735–36.

Francesco Solimena
(Nocera dei Pagani 1657–Barra 1747)

2. *Jacob and Rachel*

Canvas, 198 × 150 cm

3. *Rebecca and the Servant of Abraham*

Canvas, 202 × 150 cm
Acquisition: 1920, by purchase, (cat. 871, 870)
Latest restoration: 1963-64

These two paintings were completed around 1710 for the Venetian home of the Baglioni family on Rio Marin, and were then transferred, towards middle of that century, to the Palazzo Muti in San Cassiano, where they remained until their purchase in 1920. The modelling of the forms and vigorous chiaroscuro contrasts were surely noted by artists such as Giambattista Piazzetta and Giambattista Tiepolo during their early activity.

4. **Giambattista Tiepolo**
(Venice 1696–Madrid 1770)

Saint Joseph with the Baby Jesus and Saints Francis of Paola, Anne, Anthony and Peter of Alcantara

Canvas, 210 × 114 cm
Acquisition: 1838, following the Napoleonic suppressions, (cat. 484)
Latest restoration: 1960-61

This work was completed in the early 1740s for the church of the Benedictine monks of San Prosdocimo in Padua. It reveals the continuing influence of Piazzetta in the brownish intonation of the colour, and in the compositional structure.

5. **Giambattista Pittoni**
(Venice 1687-1767)

Annunciation

Canvas, 153 x 205 cm
Acquisition: 1807, from the old Accademia, (cat. 438)
Latest restoration: 1961

Painted in 1757 and displayed in 1777 at the Fiera della Sensa, after the death of the artist.
The work was painted for the Assembly Hall of the Accademia, in its old location at the Fonteghetto della Farina. Angeli and Marinetti also assisted with the decoration of the hall. Pittoni's emphasis seems to have been concentrated on the forms in the composition, which reveal notable stylistic virtuosity.

15

5

6

7

8

6. Giannantonio Guardi
(Vienna 1699-Venice 1760)

Herminia and Vaprinus Happen upon the Wounded Tancredi after his Duel with Argante

Canvas, 250 × 261 cm
Acquisition: 1988
(cat. 1387)

This work, recovered by Rodolfo Siviero in an English collection, is the only work by Guardi at the Accademia, and was probably part of a cycle of 13 paintings originally in a villa in Este. The painting was inspired by an edition of Tasso's *Jerusalem Delivered* with engravings by Piazzetta from around 1750-55, at the height of his maturity. The engravings are now dispersed among various museums and collections abroad. The painting depicts a scene from the 19th canto of the epic poem, in close relation to the Piazzetta drawing at the Biblioteca Reale in Turin and its related engraving. Giannantonio's interpretation incorporates a fresh chromatic scheme, with light brush strokes, while a theatrical flair accentuates the typically Rococo musicality and easy grace of the composition.

Giovan Antonio Pellegrini
(Venice 1675-1741)

7. *Sculpture*
Canvas, 142 × 132 cm

8. *Painting*
Canvas, 142 × 132 cm
Acquisition: 1959, by purchase (cat. 1320, 1319)
Latest restoration: 1959

These two *pendants* from the late 1720s depict the allegory of Painting and Sculpture. They are representative of Pellegrini's subtle elegance and refined use of colour, one of the protagonists of the international Rococo, the brother-in-law of Rosalba Carriera.

9

9. Angelo Trevisani
(Treviso? 1669-1753/55)

The Expulsion of the Merchants from the Temple

Canvas, 121 × 201 cm
Acquisition: 1912, by purchase (cat. 790)
Latest restoration: 1960

This is the draft, with notable variations, of the large painting made by the artist in 1732 for the Venetian church of Santi Cosma and Damiano on Giudecca island. After the suppressions it was transferred to Milan, and from 1818 it was kept in the parish church of Somaglia (Lodi).

10. Giandomenico Tiepolo
(Venice 1727-1804)

Abraham and the Angels

Canvas, 200 × 281 cm
Acquisition: 1807 (cat. 834)
Latest restoration: 1960

This is the last painting commissioned by the Scuola della Carità to complete the decoration of the new Chancellery which was erected in 1764. A contest was held for this purpose, whose theme turned on the *Return of the Prodigal Son* with entrants sending drafts to a Roman academy commission which included Raffaele Mengs. Giandomenico won the competition, and on March 8, 1773 he began the work for a total of 116 *zecchini* (sequins). A drawing by Giambattista at the State Museum of Berlin appears to have been a counterpart of this piece; the group of angels recalls one painted by his father of the same subject in the Prado, while the figure of Abraham is inspired by the painting in the Luna-Villahermosa collection in Madrid. There are three preparatory studies for Abraham by Giandomenico at the Museo Correr. The smoothness of the colour and the cold purity of the drawing are early reflections of neo-classical thought.

15

10

Early Works by Giambattista Tiepolo and Sebastiano Ricci

This room has the same original dimensions of the convent cell. It was remodelled by Carlo Scarpa in 1947; later, in 1959, he also designed the support for Piazzetta's *Fortune Teller*.

Giambattista Tiepolo,
Rape of Europa,
detail

Sebastiano Ricci
(Belluno 1640-Venice 1734)

1. *Diana and Calypso*

Canvas, 64 × 76 cm
Acquisition: 1988
(cat. 1383)

This work was originally in a private British collection, then to the Contini Bonacossi collection in Florence. It was purchased in 1941 by Goering, who took it to Germany where it was recovered by Rodolfo Siviero in 1948. Inspired by Ovid's *Metamorphoses*, this painting depicts the moment when Diana points at Calypso, who was guilty of having been seduced by Jove. Appearing almost neo-classical, this composition was also sketched on a sheet in the Galleries. With its elegant use of colour, the work is attributed to the English period of the artist's career, from 1712-1716.

1

2. *Bacchanal in Honour of Pan*

Canvas, 84 × 100 cm
Acquisition: 1988
(cat. 1384)

This painting, previously in the Detsy collection, passed over to the Voss collection of Wiesbaden and then to the Barsanti's in Rome. It was later exported to Germany, where it was recovered by Rodolfo Siviero in 1954. Studied in numerous drawings kept in the royal collections of Windsor and the Accademia Galleries, the piece dates to 1716, after Ricci's brief stay in Paris while returning from London. The circular movement visible in this painting renders the drunkenness of the bacchanal in honour of Pan, the deity with the horn and the goat's hooves, lover of dance, music and wine.

16

3

5

4

6

Giambattista Tiepolo
(Venice 1696–Madrid
1770)

3. *Rape of Europa*

Canvas, 100 × 135 cm
Acquisition: 1898, by
purchase (cat. 435)
Latest restoration: 1993

4. *Diana and Acteon*

Canvas, 100 × 135 cm
Acquisition: 1898,
by purchase (cat. 440)
Latest restoration: 1993

5. *Apollo and Marsyas*

Canvas, 100 × 135 cm
Acquisition: 1907,
by purchase (cat. 711)
Latest restoration: 1993

6. *Diana Discovers Calypso
Pregnant*

Canvas, 100 × 135 cm
Acquisition: 1907,
by purchase (cat. 712)
Latest restoration: 1993

On the first canvas is
depicted Europa, the
daughter of the
Phoenician king Agenor,
who was taken to Crete
by Jove disguised as a bull,
where she gave birth to
Minos. On the second
canvas is Acteon, who is
changed to a stag after
seeing Diana bathing
nude; he is then torn to
pieces by his own hunting
dogs. In the third is
represented the musical

contest between Apollo
and Pan; Midas is already
depicted with ass's ears,
the punishment he
received for not picking
Apollo as the winner.
On the last painting
Diana discovers that the
huntress Callisto has been
seduced by Zeus. Chased
away by Diana, she then
gives birth to Arcas
and is changed by Hera
into a bear. Later her son
will find her and almost
kill her, but Zeus
intervenes, changing
both into constellations.
The four paintings –
identical in format
and style – are all inspired
by Ovid's *Metamorphoses*.

Acquired a few years apart
in Belluno, the pieces were
part of a decorative series,
probably in a Belluno
palazzo. They are early
works by the artist,
from around 1720-21,
when Tiepolo was about
to abandon the dark and
dramatic tones and lighten
his palette, demonstrating
a new ability to articulate
figures within space.

7. *Allegory of Age
and Death*

Oil on copper, 115 × 90
Aquisition: 1968, donated
by A. Morassi in memory
of his son Mauro
(cat. 1347)
Latest restoration: 1996

Published by Morassi under
the title *Allegory of Old Age*
and ascribed to a date
around 1718-20, the small
painting on copper,
despite some initial
resistance, has now
been unanimously accepted
as an early work by the
painter, perhaps dating from
1715 (Gemin-Pedrocco),
still influenced by the
Dalmatian Federico
Bencovich.

16

Alessandro Longhi, Giambattista Piazzetta and Fra' Galgario

This room, like the previous Room 16, maintains the same original dimensions of the convent cell. Both rooms were remodelled by Carlo Scarpa in 1947.

Giambattista Piazzetta,
The Fortune Teller,
detail

16a

Piazzetta inspired painting. There is a preparatory sketch which carries a dedication and the date of 1745, also the year in which the painting here can be placed.

3. Giambattista Piazzetta
(Venice 1683-1754)

The Fortune Teller

Canvas, 154 × 115 cm
Acquisition: 1887, (cat. 483)
Latest restoration: 1983

Acquired from the merchant Ehrenfreund, on the back of the original canvas there was a leaf of paper with the date of 1740, written in 18th century handwriting, which was widely accepted by critics. This is one of the artist's most famous works, and is the culmination of his studies on the 'pastoral' theme begun many years earlier, first with the *Pastoral Scene* (in the Chicago Art Institute), and the *Idyll on the Beach* (Cologne, the Wallraf-Richartz Museum). Both of these paintings were commissioned by Marshal Schulenburg, and all three come from that joyful period of clear and bright colours that contemporaries defined as "lume solivo" (sunny light). This painting, among the most famous by Piazzetta, is universally called *The Fortune Teller*, a title suggested by the pose of the woman to the left who seems to point to the other woman's hand, but its interpretations vary widely: it can be seen politically, symbolically or even as an amorous initiation of the two youths to the right, or of one of them.
The fascination instilled by *The Fortune Teller* consists in its subtle grace, the sensual light that inundates the piece, the extremely refined chromatic harmony, the serene wisdom of the woman at the centre, who, in spite of her rustic garments is a "sister" of Tiepolo's heroines.

of the bourgeoisie, adding certain aspects from Caravaggio-influenced Rome. This painting dates to the beginning of the 1750s and is an important example of this kind of production, in which the scene is fixed with analytic precision and subtle irony.

2. Giuseppe Angeli
(Venice 1712-1798)

Il solletico

Canvas, 198 × 144 cm
Acquisition: 1995,
by purchase, (cat. 1459)
Latest restoration: 1995-96

This work came from the Berlin antiquities market, and passed on to the Pospisil collection in Venice. From there in 1990 it was moved to the Silvestro Gargantini collection in Milan, and was finally purchased by the State for the Accademia. Having studied Piazzetta, Angeli imitates similar compositions by this master, for example *The Fortune Teller*. The *Pastoral Scene* by Domenico Maggiotto (in the Kunsthalle in Hamburg), another *solletico* (tickle) scene, confirms the general diffusion of this kind of

1. Gaspare Traversi
(Naples, documented from c. 1722-Rome, 1770)

The Wounded Man

Canvas, 101 × 128 cm
Acquisition: 1956,
by purchase, (cat. 1316)

This piece is recorded in the Licata collection, and then in the collections of the Duke of Melito in Naples and of Italico Brass in Venice. Following a tradition begun in Naples by Giuseppe Bonito and in the wake of a Europe-wide trend, Traversi nurtures an increasingly clear vision of the daily life

16a

4. **Vittore Ghislandi, known as 'Fra' Galgario'**
(Bergamo 1655–1743)

Portrait of Count Giovanni Battista Vailetti

Canvas, 230 × 137 cm
Acquisition: 1912,
by purchase (cat. 778)
Latest restoration: 1995

Purchased from A. Olivotti through the Export Office of Florence. This piece from 1710 was previously in the collection of the Countess Rosa Piatti Lochis, belonged to her family for at least the latter half of the 19th century and bequeathed by the family of Luigi Vailetti. One of the most famous portraits by the artist, datable to the second decade of the 18th century, it constitutes a true "still life with precious fabrics". Perhaps because of his Lombard origin, Ghislandi moved away from the frivolous and formal style of international portraiture, and instead gave Count Vailetti – portrayed in the refined intimacy of his study – an interpretation which was both idealised and realistic at the same time, with the proper rigour of an illuminist.

4

5. Giulia Lama
(Venice 1681-1747)

Judith and Holofernes

Canvas, 104 × 151 cm
Acquisition: 1976, by purchase, (cat. 1345)

This painting came to the Galleries from the Export Office of Milan. Lama, who was perhaps the most independent of Piazzetta's students, is characterised by his emphasis on forms and his abilities with lighting, which are the foundational elements of his works. For the body of Holofernes, he based his interpretation on a study of a nude by Piazzetta, in the Accademia, which was from before the 1740s. This painting dates to about the same time as the drawing, from about 1730-1740. The biblical heroine is captured at the moment just prior to when she takes action, in an unusual position of prayer, and is shown along with the upturned body of Holofernes in a violent light to create a composition of intense drama and virtuosity.

5

6

6. Giuseppe Nogari
(Venice 1699-1763)

An Old Woman with a Bowl

Canvas, 52 x 41 cm
Acquisition: 1953, by donation from Francesco Pospisil, (cat. 1315)
Latest restoration: 1998

Alessandro Longhi's master, Nogari specialised in the production of "character heads" realised with chiaroscuro contrasts and counter-lighting effects, inspired by the Nordic tradition. The *Old Woman with a Bowl* dates to the beginning of the 1740s and is a virtuoso variation of the *Old Woman with a Staff* in the Gemäldegalerie in Dresden, and the *Old Woman with a Staff* in the Prado Museum.

16a

16a

Alessandro Longhi
(Venice 1733-1813)

7. The Family of Procurator Luigi Pisani

Canvas, 255 × 340 cm
Acquisition: 1979, by
purchase, (cat. 1355)
Latest restoration: 1996

On the globe is written
"Longhj", and on the
upper border of the pages
of the book below to the
right is the original
though fragmented
signature "Alessandro
Abate". Again to the lower
right, the inscription
"Opus Pietro Longi". This
work – inherited by the
Bentivoglio of Aragon

family and later by the
Nani Mocenigo family –
was carried out in 1758
together with a *pendant* (of
which a fragment remains
at the City Museum of
Belluno, and which
depicted the family of
Ermolao Alvise and
Andrea Pisani). On this
painting are shown Doge
Alvise Pisani (1664-1741)
with his son Luigi the
procurator, his wife
Paolina Gambara and four
children. surrounded by
allegorical figures
symbolising family virtues.
The two personages in the
back to the right are
probably two other

children of the Pisani
family, while the old man
dressed in black who
holds a "bussolà" (a
Venetian biscuit) towards
the boy is probably the
Abbot Giovanni
Gregoretti. The allegorical
figures around them allude
to various family virtues;
to the upper right can be
seen the villa of Stra.
Longhi emphasises the
small slices of the father
Paolo's life in Venice,
adding a psychological
investigation to make the
painting one of the most
suggestive examples of
European portraiture of
the time.

7

8. *Portrait of Carlo Lodoli*

Canvas, 128 × 94 cm
Acquisition: 1930, by
donation from Count A.
di Robilant, (cat. 908)
Latest restoration: 1994

The painting carries the
signature and name of
the subject at the upper
right: the Franciscan
monk Carlo Lodoli
(Venice, 1690-1761), the
famous theoretician of
the new architectural
rationalism, opposed to
the Baroque excesses and
a vehement critic of many
of his contemporary
architects. His pitiless
approach must have
garnered him quite a few
enemies, and in fact the
inscription expresses an
ironic criticism of him.
Longhi made more than
one portrait of this
controversial figure. The
chronology of this
particular work is
difficult, although it was
surely posthumous. It
should be from around
the end of the 1770s,
given its similarity with
the portrait of
Bartolomeo Ferracina in
Ca' Rezzonico, which is
from about 1770.

16a

8

155

Canaletto, Francesco Guardi, Giambattista Tiepolo, Pietro Longhi and Rosalba Carriera

This room was fitted between 1921 and 1923 for the display of small 18th-century paintings; in 1947 Carlo Scarpa added a small narrow gallery, with a typical Venetian floor and a single velarium on the ceiling.

Canaletto, Perspective with Portico, *detail*

1

2

3

4

Giuseppe Zais
(Canale d'Agordo 1709
-Treviso 1781)

1. *Couples near a Fountain*

Canvas, 54 × 39 cm

2. *Pierrot and Couples*

Canvas, 53 × 39 cm

3. *Concert*

Canvas, 53 × 39 cm

4. *The Swing*

Canvas, 53 × 39 cm
Acquisition: 1957, from
the Palazzo Reale, (cat.
1312, 1311, 1310, 1309)
Latest restoration: 1957

The original location of
these four small paintings
is unknown. They were
inspired by French
painting of the same era,
particularly at Watteau,
which was probably
spread in Italy through
engravings and printed
illustrations. All four
works are from the artist's
mature period.

5. Bernardo Bellotto
(Venice 1721–Warsaw
1780)

*The Beggers' Canal and the
Scuola di San Marco*

Canvas, 41 × 59 cm
Acquisition: 1856, from
the Manfrin collection,
(cat. 494)

Latest restoration: 1990
This is probably the
painting alluded to by
Ruskin when he
described himself
painting the scene from
the same viewpoint, but
in opposition to
Canaletto. Nonetheless,
by now the work is
largely attributed to
Bellotto while in his
apprenticeship in the
studio of his uncle,
Canaletto; the work dates
to around 1740.

6. **Antonio Canal,
known as 'Canaletto',**
ascribed to (Venice 1697-
1768)

*Capriccio with Ruins and
Porta Portello in Padua*

Canvas, 61 × 76 cm
Acquisition: 1988, with
the recoveries by Rodolfo
Siviero, (cat. 1385)
Latest restoration: 1993

From the Contini-
Bonacossi collection in
Florence, the work was
removed in a clandestine
operation and then
recovered by Rodolfo
Siviero. There are twenty-
two copies of this
capriccio, which received
enormous praise. The
copies are attributed to
Canaletto's and Bellotto's
circle. The version in the
Kunsthalle in Hamburg is
probably the model upon
which they were based.
The excellent version in
Venice is from Canaletto's
work around the 1760s.

5

6

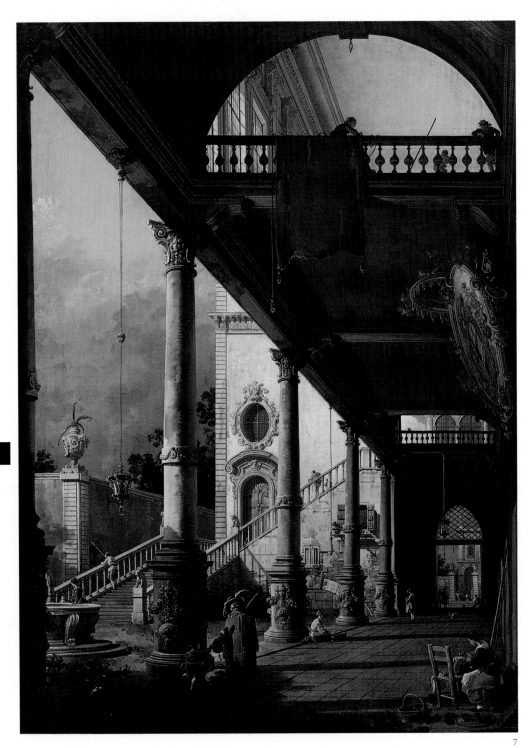

7

7. Antonio Canal, known as 'Canaletto'
(Venice 1697-1768)

Capriccio of a Colonnade

Canvas, 92 × 130 cm
Acquisition: 1807, from the old Accademia, (cat. 463)
Latest restoration: 1985

Trial work of acceptance after the artist was made professor of perspective architecture, signed and dated 1765. The *capriccio* (or imaginary view), now famous and copied many times by Canaletto himself, was exhibited in 1777 in Saint Mark's Square for the *Festa della Sensa* (The *Feast of the Ascension*). A drawing in the Albertini collection in Rome is related to the painting, and a quick sketch in Museo Correr could be an early idea for the piece.

8. Michele Marieschi
(Venice 1710-1743)

Palazzo Courtyard with Stairs

Canvas, 36 cm × 55 cm
Acquisition: 1816, bequest from Girolamo Molin, (cat. 451)
Latest restoration: 1989-90

The subject was copied in many replicas and provides evidence of the artist's scene painting experience. Inspired by the work of Marco Ricci, but with a personal interpretation employing an accentuated use of the chiaroscuro contrasts, the work appears to be from the end of the 1730s. The whole "Courtyard" series has also been attributed to Francesco Albotto, follower and continuator of Marieschi.

9. Antonio Canal, known as 'Canaletto'
ascribed by. (Venice 1697-1768)

Capriccio with Ruins and Classical Buildings

Canvas, 62 × 74 cm
Acquisition: 1988, with the recoveries by Rodolfo Siviero (cat. 1386)
Latest restoration: 1993

A *pendant* of painting n. 6 (cat. 1385) and of a similar scene. The constructions depicted in the work seem to all be of the artist's imagination, although they may bring known buildings to mind. There are sixteen replicas of this subject; the model on which these were based has been recognised as the version in the Poldi-Pezzoli museum in Milan. Comparison between the one here in Venice and the one in Milan reveals that the Venetian version is actually better, with more luminous colours and a clear descriptive analysis.

8

9

Antonio Diziani
(Venice 1737-1797)

10. *Alpine Landscape
with a Flow of Water*

Canvas, 55 × 72 cm

11. *Alpine Landscape
with a Stream and Figures*

Canvas, 55 × 72 cm
Acquisition: 1914, by
purchase, (cat. 797, 796)

Both paintings carry the
old inscription "Antonio
Diziani" on the back, and
are in fact typical examples
of the artist's landscapes.

13

14

12. **Francesco Guardi**
(Venice 1712-1793)

The Basin of Saint Mark's Square, with San Giorgio and the Giudecca

Canvas, 69 × 94 cm
Acquisition: 1903, donation from Prince John of Liechtenstein, (cat. 709)
Latest restoration: 1993

On the crate at the bottom on to the left is the signature: F. G. This is one of a many versions of theme treated numerous times by the artist. To the left the island of San Giorgio Maggiore, and to the right the Giudecca island with the demolished church of San Giovanni Battista of the Camaldolesi monks, and the church of the Zitelle. The painting maintains its expressive potential in spite of a certain graininess in the colour.
It is from no later than 1774, when the old onion-domed bell tower collapsed (still visible on the island of San Giorgio).

Marco Ricci
(Belluno 1676-Venice 1730)

13. *Landscape with Woodsmen and Knights*

Goat skin, 29 × 45 cm

14. *The Park of a Villa*

Goat skin, 30 × 44 cm
Acquisition: 1956, from Palazzo Reale, (cat. 1308, 1307)

These two *pendants* were painted in tempera on goat skin – a technique which creates the effect of extraordinary luminosity. They date to just before 1724, and were probably originally in the monastery of San Giorgio. The second painting, with its evocation of aspects of the daily work of a patrician villa, is a forerunner of the great *vedutisti* (view painters).

10

11

12

Michele Marieschi
(Venice 1710-1743)

15. *Capriccio with a Classical Arch and Goats*

Canvas, 55 × 83 cm

16. *Capriccio with a Gothic Building and an Obelisk*

Canvas, 55 × 83 cm
Acquisition: 1903, by purchase, (cat. 727, 728)

These two *pendants* are highly original and refined works. The small speckles remind the viewer of the work of Giannantonio Guardi. Other versions by the artist and his workshop exist of these two paintings, and especially of the second one.

15

16

Francesco Guardi
(Venice 1712-1793)

17. The Anconeta Island

Canvas, 32 × 51 cm
Acquisition: 1903, by
donation from M.
Guggenheim, (cat. 704)
Latest restoration: 1984

One of the late views by
Guardi, of which there is
a better version in the
Fogg Art Museum in
Cambridge. The painting
depicts the island of
Anconeta, also called the
'Madonnetta' because of
the small church located
on it. The piece
documents a small island
in front of San Giuliano
which does not exist
today; it was probably a
resting point for the trip
from the mainland to
Venice.

18. Fire at S. Marcuola

Canvas, 32 cm × 51 cm
Acquisition: 1972, by
exercise of purchase
right, (cat. 1344)
Latest restoration: 1993

This is Guardi's rendering
of a real event: the
dramatic fire at the oil
storehouse in the Ghetto,
which occurred on

November 28, 1789.
It is among the artist's
masterpieces within the
documentary style,
composed towards his
late maturity.

17

17

18

19. Giambattista Tiepolo
(Venice 1696-Madrid 1770)

Healing of a Sick Man at the Pool of Bethesda

Canvas, 62 × 45 cm
Acquisition: 1902, by purchase, (cat. 651)

An early work from around 1718-20, of excellent quality. A defect in the preparation of the canvas with oil and red ochre resulted in poor adhesion of the paint film, which is peeling away, revealing the brownish ochre behind it.

20. Jacopo Amigoni
(Naples? 1682?-Madrid, 1752)

Venus and Adonis

Canvas, 51 × 72 cm
Acquisition: 1910, by purchase, (cat. 743)

A special subject for Amigoni, who used it many times. This is a typical example of *boudoir* art which made Amigoni very wealthy, and is from around the 1750s.

17

19

21. Giambattista Tiepolo?
(Venice 1696 -Madrid 1770)

Anzia and Abrocome Meet at the Feasts of Diana

Canvas, 52 × 70 cm
Acquisition: 1911, by purchase, (cat. 740)

Originally belonged to Counts Belloni Corniani, the heirs of Francesco Algarotti. The painting was also identified as a draft for a painting by Amigoni, now lost, sent in 1744 to the court of Dresden. However, critics do not all agree with this identification, with some holding that Tiepolo could have painted Amigoni's subject for Algarotti.

20

21

22. Giambattista Pittoni
(Venice 1687-1767)

Crassus Ransacks the Temple of Jerusalem

Canvas, 54 × 72 cm
Acquisition: 1910, by purchase, (cat. 741)

Recorded in the Corniani Gallery of the Algarotti family, this is the 1743 model for the painting commissioned by Francesco Algarotti for the gallery of Augustus III in Dresden.

17

22

23

23. Sebastiano Ricci

(Belluno 1659-Venice 1734)

The Dream of Aesculapius

Canvas, 78 × 97 cm
Acquisition: 1929, by donation from Alessandro Contini, (cat. 910)
Latest restoration: 1993-94

A classic Rococo piece, the painting depicts Aesculapius, the god of medicine, with his trademark staff and snake. He appears on a cloud before a sleeping sick man. The work dates to the end of the 1710s.

17

24

24. Giambattista Tiepolo

(Venice 1696-Madrid 1770)

The Discovery of the True Cross and Saint Helena

Canvas, 51 × 49 cm
Acquisition: 1913, by purchase from Generoso Añes of Toledo, (cat. 789)
Latest restoration: 1985

This is the preparatory draft – or rather an early idea – for the large canvas by Tiepolo originally on the ceiling of the church of the Cappuccine in Castello (now in Room 11). The piece is characterised by a rapid, rotating movement that is somewhat more tranquil in the final version. Dates to around 1740.

25. Francesco Fontebasso
(Venice 1709-1769)

The Last Supper

Canvas, 70 cm × 124 cm
Acquisition: 1924, by
purchase, (cat. 880)

This piece is the *pendant*
of no. 29 (cat. 879). It is
an early work, a replica of
the painting by
Sebastiano Ricci at
Worcester College in
Oxford.

26. Alessandro Magnasco
(Genova c. 1667-Madrid
c. 1749)

Christ Adored by Two Nuns

Canvas, 58 × 43 cm
Acquisition: 1929, by
donation from Benno
Geiger, (cat. 909)

The small canvas is part
of the series of images
created for the worship
of the commissioners
who were particularly
sensitive to Franciscan
spirituality. Christ, risen
again and defeating Satan
– who can be seen
crushed under the clouds
– presents the
communion bowl to two
adoring nuns, perhaps
Saint Claire and another
Franciscan saint. The
piece dates to around
1721-23.

26

27. Giambattista Tiepolo
(Venice 1696–Madrid 1770)

The Glory of Saint Dominic

Canvas, 78 × 72 cm
Acquisition: 1922,
by purchase, (cat. 810)
Latest restoration: 1992-93

A draft painted for the competition in March of 1723 for the ceiling of the chapel of San Domenico in the Basilica of Santi Giovanni and Paolo. This contest was won by Giambattista Piazzetta.

28. Giambattista Pittoni
(Venice 1687-1767)

Mary Magdalene

Canvas, 45 x 36 cm
Acquisition: 1903,
by donation from W. Bode,
(cat. 707)

The painting dates to before 1740, and was a draft for the altar piece originally in the church of Santa Maria Maddalena in Parma, today in the city's Picture Gallery.

27

28

29. Francesco Fontebasso
(Venice 1709-1769)

Adoration of the Magi

Canvas, 70 × 123 cm
Acquisition: 1924, by
purchase, (cat. 879)

Like n. 15 (cat. 880) –
with which the piece
comprises a *pendant* – this
too is an early work,
strongly influenced by
Sebastiano Ricci, to whom
it was once attributed.

30. Giambattista Piazzetta
(Venice 1683-1754)

Christ on the Cross

Canvas, 70 × 48 cm
Acquisition: 1923, by
purchase from the convent
of Santa Maria della Fava,
(cat. 809)

Originally in the Filippini
Oratory connected to the
church of Santa Maria
della Fava. The painting
reveals great pictorial
elegance, although the
chiaroscuro contrasts are
accentuated by faults in
the technical execution.

17

Rosalba Carriera
(Venice 1675-1758)

31. *Portrait of a Young Nobleman*

Paper, 58 × 47 cm
Acquisition: 1816, by
bequest from Girolamo
Molin, (cat. 491)

With a masterful use of
pastels – which were made
for the artist in Rome by
her friend Christian Cole –
Carriera creates images
almost without any
preparatory drawing, giving
the piece unusual
luminosity thanks to her
use of a dark blue paper.
This portrait dates to 1727.

32. *Portrait of the French Consul, Le Blond*

Paper, 57 × 45 cm
Acquisition: 1888, bequest
from Vincenzo Omoboni
Astori, (cat. 490)

Father of Astori's mother, Le
Blond was the General
Consul of France in Venice.
On September 27, 1727,
Carriera wrote in her diary
that she had received 16
zecchini for the portrait. The
image of Le Blond,
confidently aware of his
status, is rendered
incorporating the influence
of Bombelli's and Cassana's
portraiture, but translated into
a ductile pastel technique.

31

32

33

34

17

33. *Portrait of a Young Woman*

Paper, 55 × 41 cm
Acquisition: 1888,
by bequest from Vincenzo
Omoboni Astori (cat. 496)

This work is by Carriera,
and there is no indication
of previous restorations,
as was recently suggested.
Although the woman was
previously identified as the
wife of Consul Le Blond,
she shows none of the
usual attributes of that
social class, and seems
rather to belong to the
bourgeoisie. The portrait
may be of Maria Felice
Tibaldi, the daughter of
the famous musician and
wife of the painter Pierre

Subleyras; the image
is very similar to the one
in a portrait made by her
husband in 1739, the year
of their marriage.

34. *Portrait of Cardinal
Melchiorre de Polignac*

Paper, 57 × 46 cm
Acquisition: 1888,
by bequest from
Vincenzo Omoboni
Astori (cat. 485),
undergoing restoration

The cardinal was a friend
of Astori's great-uncle;
the abbot Dionisio Le
Blond was his
collaborator. Both visited
Carriera many times in
Paris, and it is possible

that the portrait was
begun in 1732 while
Polignac was returning
to Paris after being in
Rome. The work was
definitely completed
by February 14, 1734,
when the Parisian
collector Jean de Julienne
wrote to Carriera in
admiration of the piece.

35. *Self-portrait*

Canvas, 31 × 25 cm
Acquisition: 1927,
through a purchase
option from the Naya
Company (cat. 907)

This painting was made
by the artist a few years
before she fell victim to

"a total loss of reason";
she would call the piece
a "tragedy", meaning
"that Rosalba would
end tragically".
Compared with the
similar subject in the
English collections,
Carriera's face appears
pained and tired, almost
foreshadowing the real
blindness that would
afflict the painter
in 1746.

35

Rosalba Carriera
(Venice 1675-1758)

36. *Portrait of a Boy*

Canvas, 34 × 27 cm
Acquisition: 1888,
bequest from Vincenzo
Omoboni Astori (cat. 445)

This work, like its
pendant *Portrait of a Girl
with a Bussolà*, is undoubtedly a portrait
of the son of the French
consul Le Blond, and
reveals an image of
exquisite grace and
gentleness. It was made in
1726, just after the
portrait of the girl.

17

36

37. Portrait of the Abbot Dionisio Le Blond

Paper, 57 × 45 cm
Acquisition: 1888, bequest from Vincenzo Omoboni Astori, (cat. 486)
Latest restoration: in progress

Dating to 1729, as a letter from the abbot to the painter would seem to indicate, this piece reveals a greater emphasis on realism.

38. Portrait of Girl with a Bussolà

Paper, 34 × 27 cm
Acquisition: 1888, by bequest from Vincenzo Omoboni Astori, (cat. 444)

As Carriera wrote in her diary, the portrait was begun on May 13, 1725, while on July 22 she adds: "received a snuff-box with ten sequins (*zecchini*) from the French ambassador", which was probably payment for the work. The pastel technique renders the tender grace of the girl perfectly, depicting her with delicate analysis in the description of the refined dress, the pink ribbon in her hair, the scarf tied around her neck, and the *bussolà* – a typical Venetian biscuit – in her hand.

39. Portrait of a Lady

Paper, 50 × 40 cm
Acquisition: 1816, bequest from Girolamo Molin, (cat. 489)

For a long time this was mistakenly held to be a self-portrait; the identification of the woman as Anna Carlotta Gauthier, the wife of painter Jacques Aved, is also unconfirmed. The work dates to the 1730s.

37

38

39

40. Giambattista Tiepolo
(Venice 1696–Madrid
1770)

*Transfer of the Holy
House from Nazareth to
Loreto*

Canvas, 126 × 86 cm
Acquisition: 1930, by
purchase, (cat. 911)
Latest restoration: 1993-94

A preparatory sketch for
the ceiling and fresco
painted by Tiepolo and
Girolamo Mengozzi,
known as Colonna in
the church of Santa
Maria di Nazareth at the
Scalzi, which was
destroyed in 1915 by an
Austrian bomb (seven

surviving fragments are
on display in Room 11).
This is probably the first
model for the
composition, for which
the artist was paid 100
zecchini on September
13, 1743. The second
model, which is more
similar to the final

version, is at the Getty
Museum in Malibu,
California. The piece
celebrates the miraculous
conveyance of the house
of Nazareth to Loreto,
where the Virgin
encountered the angel
Gabriel.

41

42

Pietro Longhi
(Venice 1701-1785)

41. *The Tailor*

Canvas, 60 × 49 cm
Acquisition: 1838, donation
from Girolamo Contarini,
(cat. 469)

In spite of the traditional
title, this is actually a group
portrait, as is shown by the
image of the Procurator
Nicolò Renier, elected in
1740, hanging on the wall.
Samaritana Dolfin, the wife
of Nicolò Renier's brother,
Girolamo, has just received
the tailor, with a
magnificent new dress; next
to her the daughter Maria
plays with the dog. Dating
to after *The Concert*,
between 1742–43, this piece
came to the Galleries from
the Contarini collection.

42. *The Concert*

Canvas, 60 × 49 cm
Acquisition: 1838, donation
from Girolamo Contarini,
(cat. 466)

Signed and dated Pietro
Longhi, 1741, this painting
is a masterpiece revealing
the transition from the
popular form derived from
Giuseppe Maria Crespi to
the more refined
'conversation piece' taken
from the French tradition.

43

The work confirms
Longhi's place as a "painter
of the Veneto nobility".
Some clergymen play cards
in a suggestive patrician
room, while the owners of
the house are arranged in an
unusual trio of only
violinist.

43. *The Chemist*

Canvas, 59 × 48 cm
Acquisition: 1835, donation
from Girolamo Contarini,
(cat. 467)

With the artist's signature
on the back, this is
probably his most famous
painting. The interior,
described in such intricate
detail that the *Nativity*
painting by Antonio
Balestra can be recognised,
a work now in a private
collection in Venice.
Longhi evokes an 18th
century chemist's shop
with extraordinary success.
The piece dates to around
the same time as *The
Rhinoceros* in Ca'
Rezzonico, from 1751.

17

44. *A Lady's Dressing-Room*

Canvas, 60 × 48 cm
Acquisition: 1838,
donation from Girolamo
Contarini, (cat. 464)

The focus of the
composition is the
splendid dress worn by
the lady, which shows
that the dressing ritual
was an important
moment in the day of
18th century Venetian
patrician women. From
around the same time as
the *Concert*.

45. *The Dancing Lesson*

Canvas, 60 × 48 cm
Acquisition: 1838,
donation from Girolamo
Contarini, (cat. 465)

A famous painting which
was made diffuse through
a counterpart engraving
by Flipart. The work
depicts one of the
fundamental aspects of
the education of young
Venetian patrician girls,
and dates to around the
1740s or 50s.

44

46. *The Fortune-Teller*

Canvas, 60 × 48 cm
Acquisition: 1838,
donation from Girolamo
Contarini, (cat. 468)

The inscription, top right
"Per Piovan/in San
Fantin/pre' Zuanne",
probably refers to the
parochial election in San
Fantin of don Giovanni
(Zuanne) Pecchion,
which occurred on
August 6, 1759, the *post
quem* date for the
completion of this piece.

17

46

45

Trial works by the Academicians and models by Antonio Canova

This hallway was constructed in the early 19th century and redesigned by Carlo Scarpa in 1953. He closed off two windows and added a single door towards the overhang. The wooden base was eliminated, the ceiling was lowered and new skylights were opened. The display case with the Canova sketches were added in 1949. Originally the room was to be used for displaying a rotation of drawings, but later trial works from the old Accademia at the Fonteghetto della Farina were added.

Antonio Maria Visentini,
Architectural Invention,
detail

1. Giuseppe Zais
(Canale d'Agordo 1709 -Treviso 1781)

Landscape with a Fountain

Canvas, 132 × 80 cm
Acquisition: 1807, from the old Accademia, (cat. 447)
Latest restoration: 1962

On the left, at the bottom, are the artist's initials. With this painting he applied, in 1765, to be accepted into the Accademia, but was not admitted until September 11, 1774.

2. Francesco Battaglioli
(Modena, c. 1720–Venice, records until 1797)

Architectural Perspective

Canvas, 131 × 56 cm
Acquisition: 1807, from the old Accademia, (cat. 461)
Latest restoration: 1987

Chosen in 1777 with other canvases from the old Accademia to be exhibited at the *Fiera della Sensa* fair in Saint Mark's Square. The painting was completed by Battaglioli

to mark his nomination to the Accademia in 1776. The inventive work reveals his talents for perspective and his familiarity with Canaletto's work.

3. Giuseppe Moretti
(originally from Val Camonica, active in Venice during the second half of the 18th century)

Perspective Study

Canvas, 130 × 56 cm
Acquisition: 1807, from the old Accademia, (cat. 471)
Latest restoration: 1987

Displayed at the *Fiera della Sensa* in 1777, this painting was submitted by Moretti for his entrance into the Accademia in 1776. Canaletto's influence is evident, especially in the figures that recall those in the *Campo San Giacomo at Rialto* in the State Museum of Berlin.

4. Pietro Gaspari
(Venezia 1720–1785)

Architectural Perspective

Canvas, 131 × 79 cm
Acquisition: 1807, from the old Accademia, (cat. 470)
Latest restoration: 1987

To the lower left on the base is the signature and the date of 1775. This is the "pièce de reception" for Gaspari's acceptance into the Accademia, and is a good representation of virtuosity of the "perspective" trend in the 1700s.

5. Antonio Joli
(Modena, c. 1700-Naples, 1777)

Perspective with Ancient Baths

Canvas, 130 × 93 cm
Acquisition: 1807, from the old Accademia, (cat. 450)
Latest restoration: 1987

"Pièce de reception" for Joli's acceptance into the Accademia, to which he was elected on February 13, 1756, this is a typical example of the artist's painting. After working as a scene painter in

Modena until about 1740, he went to Venice to become one of the major exponents of "perspective" painting, working also in Germany, London and Madrid.

6. **Antonio Maria Visentini**
(Venice 1688-1782)

Architectural Invention

Canvas, 135 × 94 cm
Acquisition: 1807, from the old Accademia, (cat. 448)

The signature is written at the left on the edge of the balustrade. A group of architects intent on measuring the ruins of an ancient building stand in a portico that recalls Veronese and Palladio. Their very presence, along with the drawing tools, the plumb line, Palladio's *Trattato* at easy reach, all allude to the teaching of architectural perspective as an essential element of painting. The work was connected with the institution of the Perspective Chair at the Accademia, to which Visentini was appointed in 1764, but which was only confirmed in 1772. The work was probably completed after this date, and is recorded in 1777, when it was displayed at the *Fiera della Sensa*.

4

5

18

6

183

7. Domenico Fedeli, known as 'Maggiotto'
(Venice 1713-1794)

Allegory of the Academy

Canvas, 130 × 92 cm
Acquisition: 1807, from the old Accademia, (cat. 443)
Latest restoration: 1960

The signature is to the lower right. This painting was probably donated to the Accademia in 1763. The artist was admitted to the Accademia in 1756; this work is significant for its refined academic nature, in which Maggiotto effectively translates the teachings of Piazzetta.

8. Michelangelo Morlaiter
(Venezia 1729-1806)

Venice Awards the Fine Arts

Canvas, 131 × 183 cm
Acquisition: 1807, from the old Accademia, (cat. 425)
Latest restoration: 1960

Displayed at the *Fiera della Sensa* in 1777, the work had most likely been donated to the Accademia in 1756 by Morlaiter when he was admitted. The figure of Venice is depicted awarding prize-medals to Painting, Sculpture and Architecture. The 'academic' subject echoes a neo-classical aspect.

9. Francesco Maggiotto
(Venice 1750-1805)

Allegory of Painting

Canvas, 130 × 115 cm
Acquisition: 1807, from the old Accademia, (cat. 442)

The signature is to the right on the sheet under the palette. The work was the obligatory donation made by the artist in 1769 for his election into the Accademia in 1768. While the seated woman symbolises Painting, the standing woman is an allegory for Nature. The boy to the right represents Drawing. The influence of new neo-classical theories is evident in the work.

10. Pietro Longhi
(Venice 1702-1785)

The Philosopher Pythagoras

Canvas, 130 × 91 cm
Acquisition: 1807, from the old Accademia, (cat. 479)

The signature is written at the lower left. The title is the one used by Pietro's son Alessandro for the engraving made of this painting. The work was completed as an entrance piece for the Accademia, which selected Longhi in its first group of students in February of 1756. Between the end of 1762 and the first months of 1763, it appears that – following their recall in May of 1761

– on November 14 of 1762 it was decided to send the canvases back to Longhi and to the other painters who had not yet completed the work required by the statute, with the injunction that the works were to be completed within six months. Longhi's position as an instructor on painting nudes evidently influenced his choice of subject.

11. Francesco Zuccarelli
(Pitigliano, 1702-Florence, 1788/89)

Landscape with John the Baptist

Canvas, 132 × 94 cm
Acquisition: 1807, from the old Accademia, (cat. 458)
Latest restoration: 1960

Zuccarelli was elected into

7

9

8

10

the Accademia on January 16 of 1763, and at the same time was also chosen to be an instructor. The painting was originally in the old Accademia, and must have been completed immediately after his appointment. Although the figure of John the Baptist appears conventional, the landscape reveals intense pictorial accents.

11

12. **Pierantonio Novelli**
(Venice 1729-1804)

Drawing, Colour and Invention

Canvas, 130 × 132 cm
Acquisition: 1807, from the old Accademia, (cat. 762)
Latest restoration: 1993

At the bottom-right is the inscription with the signature and date of 1776. Admitted into the Accademia in 1768, Novelli submitted this neo-classical inspired work in 1771 and revised it again in 1776.

13. **Alessandro Longhi**
(Venice 1733-1813)

Painting and Merit

Canvas, 128 × 93 cm
Acquisition: 1807, from the old Accademia, (cat. 493)
Latest restoration: 1958

The signature is painted on the spine of the book. This allegorical painting refers to the artist's acceptance into the Accademia in 1759 but dates to the end of the 1770s.
The artist made an engraving of the painting and dedicated it to John Udny, the English Consul in Venice in 1761 and from 1773-75.

13

18

12

Antonio Canova
(Possagno 1757-Venice 1822)

14. *Fighters*

Terracotta, 30 × 31 cm
Acquisition: 1807, from the old Accademia, (cat. 549)
Latest restoration: 1979

The signature is painted on the base. With this group from 1775, Canova won second prize at the first sculpture competition held by the Accademia. The subject is taken from the old plaster copy in the Filippo Farsetti collection (which was generously made available to the students); the original is in the Uffizi in Florence. The small terracotta was made when Canova was only 18 years old, and established him as the last great exponent of 18th century Venetian figurative culture.

14

18

16

15. *Apollo*

Terracotta, height 61 cm
Acquisition: 1807, from the
old Accademia, (cat. 550)
Latest restoration: 1987

The signature is painted
on the base. Antonio
Canova submitted this
sculpture on March 30,
1779 to apply for
membership of the
Accademia; he was
unanimously accepted on
April 5, 1779. With this
sculpture, Canova
demonstrates that in spite
of his 18th century
education, he was also
quite familiar with the
work of Bernini. Many of
Bernini's models were in
the Farsetti collection,
which Canova frequented
assiduously.

16. *Pietà*

Clay, 21 × 34 cm
Acquisition: 1911,
by purchase, (cat. 552)
Latest restoration: 1980

The signature is engraved
on the base at the centre.
After Canova died, this
work was passed down to
his student Baruzzi who
donated it in 1831 to the
clergyman Gardenghi.
Gardenghi's brother gave
it to Cardinal Baruffi, the
Bishop of Imola, who
then left it to his heirs.
A late work based on a
common subject, it
nonetheless maintains the
quick spirit of invention
found in the artist's
earlier works.

18

15

Bartolomeo Montagna, Giovanni Agostino da Lodi and Boccaccio Boccaccino

This is a corridor which connects with Rooms 20 and 21, showing 15ᵗʰ-century "story" cycles. The platform at the back with the sash window from which one can admire the view of the Palladio convent, was designed by Carlo Scarpa in 1947.

Marco Marziale, Supper in Emmaus, *detail*

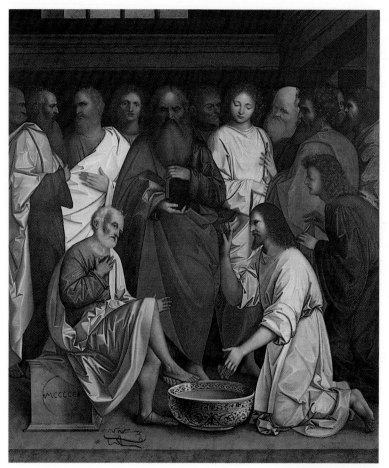

1. **Giovanni Agostino da Lodi**

(Active from the end of the 15th century, with records from until c. 1520)

Washing of the Feet

Panel, 132 × 111 cm
Acquisition: 1856,
purchase from the Manfrin collection, (cat. 599)
Latest restoration: 1991-92

The date of 1500 is painted on Saint Peter's stool. The work is inspired by the arrangement of the heads and the physical characterisations of the *Last Supper* by Leonardo da Vinci, and there are also numerous references to Bramantino. The original location of the work is unknown, but it was probably made for Venice since it is well known and was often imitated there.

2

3

4

2. **Pietro de Saliba**?

(active at the end of the 15th and the beginning of the 16th centuries)

Christ at the Column

Panel, 40 × 33 cm
Acquisition: 1856, by purchase from the Manfrin collection, (cat. 589)
Latest restoration: 1993

This painting was part of a group of works depicting the bust of Christ crowned with thorns and against a column with a rope around his neck; the works were all based on a model by Antonello which may be his *Christ,* now at the Louvre.

3. **Antonello de Saliba**

(Messina c. 1467-c. 1535)

Annunciation

Panel, 47 × 34 cm
Acquisition: 1812, following the Napoleonic suppressions, (cat. 590)
Latest restoration: 1993

Originally in the Sala dell'Ante-Collegio at the Doge's Palace, the work was part of a group of paintings donated to the Republic by Bertucci Contarini. Although it was long believed to be the work of Antonella da Messina, it is instead a copy of the *Annunciation* by the master in the

Galleria Nazionale in Palermo, completed around 1476-1477. The presence of Venetian motifs derived from Bellini and Montagna confirmed that the piece was by Antonello de Saliba (the son of a brother-in-law of Antonello da Messina), who resided in Venice from 1480-1497.

4. **Marco Basaiti**?

(Venice, 1470/75-1530)

Saint Jerome

Panel, 54 × 42 cm
Acquisition: 1816, bequest from Girolamo Molin, (cat. 107)
Latest restoration: 1993

A work for private devotion, the subject was copied many times by Basaiti; this may be from the artist's later period.

5. **Marco Basaiti**, attr.

(Venice, 1470/75-post 1530)

Christ between Two Angels

Panel, 39 × 103 cm
Acquisition: 1812-14, following the Napoleonic suppressions, (cat. 108)
Latest restoration: 1993

This piece came to the Accademia galleries together with *Saint James the Apostle* and *Saint Anthony the Abbot* from the convent of Santa Maria dei Miracoli. It is traditionally attributed to Basaiti, and the most recent restoration revealed its extraordinarily high quality. The representation of Christ's dead body – typical of Venetian painters – is deeply rooted in Byzantine iconography. Similarities are also in evidence between this work and Carpaccio's *Mourning of the Dead Christ* in the Berlin State Museum.

19

5

6

7

8

6. Bartolomeo Cincani, known as 'Montagna'
(Vicenza c. 1449–1523)

Saint Peter

Panel, 60 × 39 cm
Acquisition: 1971, by purchase, (cat. 1343)
Latest restoration: 1979

On the scroll held in the mouth of the dog is written "esto fidelis" (be faithful). Because of its affinity with the frescos in the Verona church of Santi Nazaro e Celso, the work has been attributed to Mantegna since 1871, when it was recorded in the Papafava collection in Padua. The painting dates to around 1505. The

work reveals the artist's extraordinary ability to bring together the human figure, architecture and landscape. The influence of Antonello da Messina is enriched with aspects inspired by Giovanni Bellini, especially evident in the enchanting background of the Veneto mainland: among the various buildings one can recognise the façade of the Duomo of Vicenza and the Arena of Pola.

Jacopo Parisati, known as 'da Montagnana'
(records from 1458–Padua, 1499)

7. *Herald Angel*

Panel, 185 × 74 cm

8. *Annunciation*

Panel, 185 cm × 76 cm
Acquisition: 1812, following the Napoleonic suppressions, (cat. 606, 608)
Latest restoration: 1984

Originally in the church of Monte Artone (Padua), these paintings must once have formed a single painting. A central part measuring about 110 cm appears to have been cut out, evident also from the interruption of the

bed with the red canopy. Vasari (1550) also notes that "il Montagnana […] fece in Padova a Santa Maria di Monte Artone una tavola nella chiesa" ("Montagnana […] painted a panel in the church of Santa Maria di Monte Artone in Padua"). The work, which was completed between 1494 and 1497, represents the artist's translation of the teachings of Mantegna into a more refined decorativism.

9. Boccaccio Boccaccino
(Ferrara? before August 22, 1466–Cremona, c. 1524/25)

Marriage of Saint Catherine, with Saints Rose, Peter and John the Baptist, The Announcement to the Shepherds, The Flight into Egypt and The Magi on Horseback

Panel, 87 × 143 cm
Acquisition: 1838, donation from Girolamo Contarini, (cat. 600)
Latest restoration: 1993

The signature is at the lower right. The work was completed at the end of the artist's stay in Venice (1506), with many elements taken from Bellini, Carpaccio and Giorgione, and even some echoes of the *Madonna of the Rosary* by Dürer, displayed in 1506 in the church of San Bartolomeo.

9

10

11

12

Marco Basaiti
(Venice, 1470/75–post 1530)

10. *Saint James the Apostle*

Panel, 114 × 35 cm

11. *Saint Anthony the Abbot*

Panel, 114 × 35 cm
Acquisition: 1812-14,
following the Napoleonic
suppressions, (cat. 68/A, 68)
Latest restoration: 1993

The two panels signed
"Marcus and Basait. p."
("Basaiti painted") on their
respective pedestals appear
to be of different quality, but
still similar in style to Marco
di Oggiono, who was called
to make some paintings for
the Milanesi confraternity at
the Frari in 1497 and 1498,
for whom Basaiti was also
completing the large altarpiece of Saint Ambrose after
the death of Alvise Vivarini.

12. Marco Marziale
(records from 1493 to 1507)

Supper in Emmaus

Panel, 122 × 141 cm
Acquisition: 1838, donation
from Girolamo Contarini,
(cat. 76)
Latest restoration: 1993

The signature and date (1506)
are on a scroll on the leg of
the table. The iconographic
source of the subject, with its
Dürer-inspired details, must
have been the lost *Supper in
Emmaus* by Giovanni Bellini
mentioned by Vasari (1568) in
the Giorgio Cornaro
collection, known now from
the engraving made of it by

Pietro Monaco and the copy
(made with collaborators) in
the Church of San Salvador.
Another variation was
painted by Marziale in 1507,
now in the State Museum in
Berlin.

**13. Anonymous Veneto
painter from the
beginning of the 16th
century**

*Apparition of the Crucifixes
of Mount Ararat in the Church
of Sant'Antonio in Castello*

Canvas, 121 cm × 174 cm
Acquisition: 1838, from the
warehouse of *Commenda*
following the Napoleonic
suppressions, (cat. 91)

Originally in the Church of
Sant'Antonio in Castello, the
work depicts the vision seen
by Francesco Ottoboni, the

prior of the convent, when he
invoked the aid of the Martyrs
of Mount Ararat (Room 2,
cat. 89) during a plague in
1511. The Martyrs appeared to
him in a dream entering in a
procession into the church
lead by Saint Peter. The
interior, with the wooden
'barco', or nuns' gallery, the ex
voto, the altar and the
polyptychs offers us an
interesting image of a Venetian
church at the beginning of the
1500s – still Gothic in style,
but undergoing remodelling.
It was originally attributed to
Carpaccio (Boschini, 1664),
but this attribution has recently
been called into question. In
effect, the general repainting
on the work – which does
however essentially keep to the
drawing underneath – makes
any critical evaluation difficult.

19

13

"Miracles of the Relic of the Cross"

Vittore Carpaccio,
Miracle of the Relic of
the Cross at the Rialto
Bridge, *detail*

This room was already constructed in 1940. Seven years later
the canvases with the "Miracles of the Cross" were placed here
provisionally; in 1959-60 Carlo Scarpa completed the arrangement,
which has remained practically unchanged ever since. The cycle
originally served to adorn the walls of the Albergo Room or the
Cross Room in the Scuola di San Giovanni Evangelista, where there
is still a relic of the Holy Cross on display, donated to the guild in
1369 by Filippo de Mezióres, the Great Chancellor of the kingdom
of Cyprus. There were originally ten canvases, including *The Miracle
of the Vendramin Ships* by Pietro Perugino, completed in 1494.
Unfortunately only eight are on display at the Accademia; Perugino's
canvas – composed while he was in Venice working in the Doge's
Palace – was destroyed and replaced in 1588. The most detailed
record on these canvases is a pamphlet from 1590 which describes
the "Miracles", supplying the artist's name and year of completion
of the paintings. The Scuola di San Giovanni Evangelista was
suppressed by Napoleonic decree in 1806, and the paintings were
delivered to the Accademia in 1820; they were displayed separately
at various times until they were finally consolidated in 1947.

1. Vittore Carpaccio
(Venice? c. 1460-1525/26)

Miracle of the Relic of the true Cross at the Rialto Bridge or *The Heading of the Possessed Man*

Canvas, 371 × 392 cm
Acquisition: 1820, following the Napoleonic suppressions, (cat. 566)
Latest restoration: 1990-91

This canvas was completed in 1494 for the east wall of the Albergo to the right of the altar, and narrates the miraculous healing of a possessed man. The work was obtained by Francesco Querini – the patriarch of Grado – through the reliquary of the sacred cross. In 1544, after hearing the opinion of "prudente messer Tizian pictor" ("the sagacious painter Titian"), a part was cut at the bottom left near the opening of the door which led to the "Albergo Nuovo", built during this period. The gap was then arbitrarily integrated. The artist synthesises three fundamental moments: the procession on the bridge, the entrance of the patriarch, and the miracle which takes place on the loggia. But even this event is overshadowed by the representation of the city itself. The bridge is still the wooden one constructed in 1458, with the drawbridge part at the centre to allow larger boats to pass. This collapsed in 1524, and was replaced by the present one made of stone. On the left can be seen the emblem of the Storione Albergo and the loggia, where the market's patrons would gather. On the right, the Fondaco dei Tedeschi, which was destroyed by fire in 1505, Ca' da Mosto with its portico which still exists today, the campanile of San Giovanni Cristostomo and the one of Santi Apostoli, rebuilt in 1672. The contrast with the analytic realism of the other canvases further reveals Carpaccio's descriptive abilities and his emphasis on chromatics.

2. Giovanni Mansueti
(records from 1485-1526/27)

The Miraculous Healing of the Daughter of Benvegnudo

Canvas, 361 × 299 cm
Acquisition: 1820, following the Napoleonic suppressions, (cat. 562)
Latest restoration: 1990

This work illustrates the miraculous event that took place in 1414, when the daughter of Benvegnudo, who had been immobile since birth, was miraculously healed when touched by three candles that her father had placed near the relic. Completed after 1502, this canvas has great historical interest, and recalls techniques employed by Carpaccio on his *Saint Ursula Cycle* (Room 21), but also imitated by other artists, such as Paolo Veronese, who will mimic the 'dead stairs' and the arcades framing the narration in his *Christ in the House of Levi* (Room 10, cat. 203).

3. Gentile Bellini
(Venice 1429-1507)

Miracle of the Relic of the Cross on San Lorenzo Bridge

1

Canvas, 326 × 435 cm
Acquisition: 1820,
following the Napoleonic
suppressions, (cat. 568)
Latest restoration: 1989–90

At the centre are the
signature and date (1500).
According to legend,
between 1370 and 1382,
during a procession to
the church of San
Lorenzo, the relic
accidentally fell into the
canal, and only the Great
Guardian Andrea
Vendramin could grab it.
The painting is also
interesting for its
depiction of the urban
scene. To the left Caterina
Cornaro and her ladies
witness the scene, while
the five people kneeling
to the right have been
identified as members of
the painter's family, but it
is more likely that they
are high ranking
members of the Scuola.

2

3

Gentile Bellini
(Venice 1429-1507)

4. *Miraculous Healing of Pietro de' Ludovici*

Canvas, 368 × 263 cm
Acquisition: 1820,
following the Napoleonic
suppressions, (cat. 563)
Latest restoration: 1992

The signature – not the original – is on an inscription on the steps, repeating an ancient tradition. It is unclear if the graft on the lower part of the work – rather rough and repainted – was in relation to the placement of a doorway. The work depicts how Pietro de' Ludovici was healed of his quartan fever after touching a candle that had been near the relic of the saint he was worshipping. The painting was probably completed in 1501 using drawings by Gentile's father Jacopo, and with extensive graphic work by Gentile himself.

5. *Procession in Saint Mark's Square*

Canvas, 373 × 745 cm
Acquisition: 1820,
following the Napoleonic
suppressions, (cat. 567)
Latest restoration: 1988–89

At the bottom in the centre of the painting can be read the date 1496 and the artist's signature. Two large grafts at the ends of the lower part probably correspond to two doorways on the front wall of the altar (Ridolfi 1648); they were filled when the painting was moved to opposite the windows after the 17th century remodelling project by Massari. The first of Gentili's paintings for the cycle, it depicts the procession taking place in Saint Mark's Square on the Feast of Saint Mark. All the schools participated in this event with their respective relics. In particular, the painting describes the event that took place on April 25, 1444, when the Brescian merchant Jacopo de' Salis prayed for and received help for his gravely wounded son. But this miracle is described with less attention than the square itself, however, which is shown here as it appeared before the changes made to it in the 16th century. The Basilica still glisters with its original mosaics, of which only one exists today. The arches and the Porta della Carta (the main door) radiate with gold and various colours. To the right, next to the ancient campanile appears the Orseolo Hospice, demolished about 50 years later when Sansovino redesigned the Square, here still with its pink brick paving and built the Procuratie Nuove.

4

20

5

6

6. Benedetto Rusconi, known as 'Diana'
(Venice c. 1460-1525)

Miracle of the Holy Cross

Canvas, 371 × 150 cm
Acquisition: 1820,
following the Napoleonic
suppressions, (cat. 565)
Latest restoration: 1990

This painting depicts an
episode that took place
on March 10, 1480, when
the son of Ser Alvise
Finetti was healed after
falling from a loft. The
work reveals the influence
of the most advanced
artists of the time,
especially Giorgione and
Lotto, and was probably
completed by 1510.

7. Lazzaro Bastiani
(Venice c. 1425/30-1512)

*Offering of the Relic of the
Cross to the Members of the
Scuola di San Giovanni
Evangelista*

Canvas, 324 × 441 cm
Acquisition: 1820,
following the Napoleonic
suppressions, (cat. 561)
Latest restoration: 1992

The painting shows
Filippo de Mezières
offering the miraculous
relic. The episode is
depicted from the
exterior, and provides a
valuable testimony of
buildings which were
later modified or
destroyed. We can
recognise the old façade
of the church of San
Giovanni Evangelista
with its portico which
was later demolished. To
the left on the side of the

Scuola can be seen the
circular windows – the
existence of which recent
restoration projects have
also confirmed – and the
raising of the large hall by
about 2 metres, which
occurred in 1495. In this
same year, according to
the 1590 pamphlet (see
the introduction to the
room), Bastiani painted
this work, probably
immediately after the
alterations.

8. Giovanni Mansueti
(records from 1485-1526/27)

*Miracle of the Relic of the
Cross in Campo San Lio*

Canvas, 322 × 463 cm
Acquisition: 1820,
following the Napoleonic
suppressions, (cat. 564)
Latest restoration: 1990

On the inscription held by
the person on the left
bringing a hand towards his
hat – probably a self-portrait
– can be read the signature
of the painter, who
considered himself a disciple
of Bellini. The extraordinary
event occurred in 1474
during the funeral of a
member of the confraternity
who had not had enough
faith in the relic; the cross
became incredibly heavy
and had to be entrusted to
the parish priest of San Lio.
Probably painted in 1494,
Mansueti must have used a
preparatory drawing by
Gentile Bellini, now in the
Uffizi. The writing on the
scroll at the far right of the
side of the church is curious:
"Casa da fitar ducati 5"
("House for rent, 5 ducats").

20

7

20

8

Vittore Carpaccio's "Legend of Saint Ursula"

In this room, which once held the collection of Girolamo Contarini, the *Saint Ursula* cycle by Carpaccio was installed between 1921 and 1923. From 1959-60 Carlo Scarpa remodelled the room, lowering the paintings, which he supported and surrounded by a strip of light oak with a thin gilt border.

The altarpiece, set slightly back and illuminated from the side by a new source of light, was separated from the canvases by wooden screens. The paintings used to decorate the walls of the Scuola di Sant'Orsola, a religious confraternity founded in the 14th century at the basilica of Santi Giovanni e Paolo. Many Venetian aristocrats belonged to the confraternity, including the Loredan family as well as numerous members of the Compagnia della Calza ("Company of the Stocking"), a sort of club set up by young men, most of them from the nobility, who chose to combine their forces in order to amuse themselves and wore stockings quartered in different colors or magnificently embroidered as an emblem. The pictorial decoration represents the story of Ursula, one of the stock of legends of medieval Europe collected in the 13th century by the Dominican Jacobus de Voragine in a compendium called the *Legenda Aurea*. Various compilations were published, culminating in Nicola de' Minerbi's Venetian edition of 1475. Carpaccio draws freely on this source, embellishing it with references to dogal ceremonies, theatrical performances and contemporary festivals and weaving it together with the story of Wilhelma, daughter of the king of England and bride of the king of Hungary. The dates on the giant canvases range from 1490 to 1495, but their execution must have taken several years longer, at least as far as the "Embassies" are concerned, given that the clock of St. Mark's, not inaugurated until February 1, 1499, appears in the *Arrival of the Ambassadors*. With the abolitions the works were transferred to the Gallerie dell'Accademia, where they can be seen today in their original sequence, while the Scuola, whose outer walls are still visible on the exterior, was later incorporated into the house of the canons of Santi Giovanni e Paolo.

Vittore Carpaccio, The Arrival of the English Ambassadors (at the court of the King of Brittany), *detail*

Vittore Carpaccio
(Venice? c. 1460-before 1526)

1. *The Arrival of the Ambassadors*

Canvas, 278 × 589 cm
Acquisition: 1812, following the Napoleonic suppressions (cat. 572)
Latest restoration: 1983

At the lower centre is the inscription: "op. victoris/carpatio/veneti". The works do not observe the logical sequence of the story, which actually begins with this canvas. The piece condenses three scenes, set off by three architectural elements:

the arrival of the ambassadors at the court of Brittany and the presentation of the Prince Hereus's marriage proposal; Ursula in her room relates to her father the marriage conditions she requires while the nurse waits at the foot of the stairs. She, like the young man in a red toga at the far left, frames the episode of the embassies, which together with the next two canvases covered an entire wall of the Scuola, introducing a long "secular" lead-up to the religious core of the story. In fact the

luxurious surroundings of the courts of Brittany and Anglia were suitable settings for portraits of the members of the confraternity and able to satisfy their desire to celebrate their own status. As on the canvas with the *Meeting and the Departure of the Betrothed* (n. 4), at the centre is a person with the emblem on his sleeve of the Compagnia della Calza degli Ortolani, a guild of pleasure-seeking nobles. A part of the lower area of the painting was cut for a door, possibly in 1647. On this occasion, the face of a page-boy

was probably covered, to the right, which the tampering severed from its body and which the latest restoration brought to light. The building in the centre is inspired by the Temple of Jerusalem, from xylographies by Reeuwich, while the influence of Perugino, who was in Venice in 1494, is evident in the arches to the left. Preparatory drawings are kept at Christ Church Library in Oxford, the Museo Nazionale in La Valletta, the British Museum in London and the British Museum in Stockholm.

21

2. *Dismissal
of the Ambassadors*

Canvas, 281 × 252 cm
Acquisition: 1812,
following the Napoleonic
suppressions (cat. 573)
Latest restoration: 1984

At the lower left is the
inscription: "victoris car/
veneti/opus". The
extraordinary Lombard
styled interior is an
excellent example of
perspective science and
chromatic awareness.
Ursula's father concludes
the diplomatic

negotiations, consigning
the reply for the King
of England's to the
ambassadors. It is one
of the most complex
canvases in the cycle,
in which a calculated
abstraction and an equally
deliberate absence of
analysis of the figures'
features tend to lend
emphasis to the space and
the architecture. The
cutaway of the splendid
hall, with its inlaid
marbles, recalls the
contemporary
architecture of Codussi

and Pietro and Tullio
Lombardo.
The ceremony, inspired
by the ones held in the
Doge's Palace, is recorded
by the scrivener on the
right, who thus takes
on the role of chronicler.
The interest in space
and neglect of portraiture
suggests that the canvas
was not painted at the
time of the other two
embassies but closer
to the *Dream of Ursula*,
dated 1495.

21

2

3. *The Return of the Ambassadors*

Canvas, 297 × 526 cm
Acquisition: 1812,
following the Napoleonic
suppressions (cat. 574)
Latest restoration: 1983

At the lower left is the
inscription: "victoris/ca
… tio/veneti/opus",
and on the base of the
pennant is an indication
of a restoration in 1623.
The last of the
negotiations: the return
home of the English
messengers with Ursula's
reply is announced near a
pier by a small page-boy
and by a 'steward', whose
job it was to introduce
the ambassadors to the
Doge's banquet to the
accompaniment of
musicians. The ceremony
is thus taken from the one
in use in the Venetian
Republic. Here, history
and news overlap,
evidenced by the young
English messenger
advancing to the left with
the insignia of the
Venetian Compagnia della
Calza society. The young
man viewed from behind
who seems to mark the
ideal center of the
composition may be
Prince Ethereus himself,
come down to meet the
ambassadors.
The story unfolds in an
urban setting that, while
it is not Venice, offers
constant reminders
of it (such as the two
towers on the left,
resembling those
of the arsenal) following
a logic that would
become typical of the
18th-century *capriccio*.

3

4. Meeting and Departure of the Betrothed

Canvas, 279 × 610 cm
Acquisition: 1812, following the Napoleonic suppressions (cat. 575)
Latest restoration: 1983-84

At the base of the pennant on an inscription are the signature and date of 1495: "victoris carpatioi/veneti-opus/MCCCCLXXXXV". This canvas is divided into three episodes: the prince takes leave of his parents before departing; the betrothed couple bid farewell to the king and queen, and finally they set sail on the ships which will bring them to Rome. In the background are shown the locations of the story: on the left is medieval England, while on the right is Renaissance Brittany, with the tower of the Knights of Rhodes and the tower of Saint Mark in Crete, taken from woodcuts by Reeuwich (1486). These buildings would seem to confirm the hypothesis that the story of Ursula alludes to that of Caterina Cornaro, the queen of Cypress. The two youths at the centre are members of the Compagnia della Calza. The seated one has the emblem of the Ortolani or the Zardinieri on his sleeve, and the initials F.Z. (Fratres Zardinieri), and on a legging the initials S.A. (Societas Amicorum). The standing one holds a scroll on which can be read the letters: "n. l. d. d. v. v. g. v. i.", which stand for "nicolaus laurentanus donum dedit ursulae virginis gloriosa virginibusque inclitis". It is thus likely that the commissioner – at least of this work – was Nicolò Loredan (Gentili).

21

4

5. *The Dream of Ursula*

Canvas, 273 × 267 cm
Acquisition: 1812,
following the Napoleonic
suppressions, (cat. 578)
Latest restoration: 1984

On the inscription at the foot of the bed is the apocryphal inscription, but which surely respects the original version: "victor carp/f/ MCCCCLXXXXV". This is the most damaged canvas, so much so that it was only exhibited in 1852 in order to ensure the unity of the cycle. Here Ursula receives the announcement of martyrdom from an angel while she sleeps in her room. This work reveals a strong Flemish influence, with one of the most suggestive interiors of Renaissance painting. The light shed by the dawn shows all the objects in the room, laden with symbolic significance, such as the myrtle and clove plants on the biforate window which allude to conjugal love and faithfulness. On the base of the statue of Hercules above the door is the inscription "diva f. av. /st. a" (divine announcements are propitious), indicating that the prophesy is actually favourable, in spite of its apparent dramatic nature.
A beautiful preparatory drawing is at the Uffizi in Florence, and shows an additional two biforate windows in the back wall.

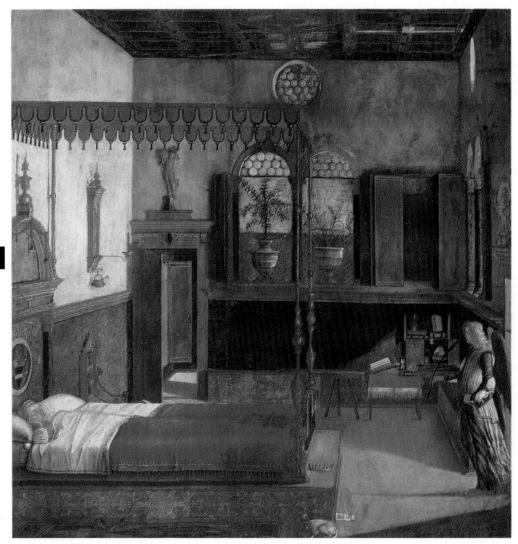

21

5

6. *The Pilgrims Meet the Pope Under the Walls of Rome*

Canvas, 279 × 305 cm
Acquisition: 1812, following the Napoleonic suppressions, (cat. 577)
Latest restoration: 1984

On the scroll is the inscription: "victoris/carpatio-veneti/opus". After a long voyage, the pilgrims have reached the gates of Rome where they meet the Pope before the Castle of Sant'Angelo, in accordance with an old diplomatic tradition "for important visitors arriving on the via Aurelia" (Zorzi). The pontefice decides to join the royal entourage after the baptism of Hereus and the coronation of the couple. The ceremony replicates a Doge's procession, as indicated by the umbrella – a typical attribute of the highest city authorities of Venice. Carpaccio was probably influenced by a Giovanni Bellini painting from the lost cycle with the stories of Alexander III in the Doge's Palace. The figure in the red toga to the right of the pope – a *didascalos*, someone who would point out the more salient elements in plays – has been identified as the Venetian humanist Ermolao Barbaro, who died in the Republic's disfavour in 1493; this fact makes it unlikely that the artist would portray him before that date.

6

7. Arrival in Cologne

Canvas, 279 × 254 cm
Acquisition: 1812,
following the Napoleonic
suppressions, (cat. 579)
Latest restoration: 1984

To the lower left on a
scroll is the inscription:
"op. victoris/carpatio/
veneti–MCCCCLXXXX.
m/septembris" (1490, in
September). This is surely
the first painting made by
the artist, evident not only
because of the date, but
also because of the
apparent difficulty in
articulating the
simultaneous
representation of many
subjects in the available
space. It was probably
made smaller – especially
at the right, where the
gates of Cologne were
entirely visible, as in the
print by Giovanni del Pian
(1785). The pilgrim's ships
are shown with Ursula
and the Pope
distinguishable on the first,
as they arrive in Cologne
to find that the city is
under siege by the Huns.
In the foreground a

7

8

warrior reads the message sent by some traitorous Roman princes warning the barbarians of their arrival. The effect of the galley that dominates the scene, a typical merchant transport ship, is truly extraordinary. The scene is taken from an engraving in the *Filocolo* by Boccaccio in the Neapolitan edition of 1475, confirmation of Carpaccio's vast knowledge of the illustrated books in his possession, and of his original ability to transpose the images.

8. *Martyrdom of the Pilgrims and the Funeral of Ursula*

Canvas, 271 × 560 cm
Acquisition: 1812, following the Napoleonic suppressions, (cat. 580)
Latest restoration: 1984

On the base of the column is the inscription with the date 1493 and the signature: "victoris/carpatio/veneti-opus/MCCCCLXXX/XIII". The column divides the two moments of the event, and carries on it the coat of arms of the Loredan family, who commissioned the work. On the left the massacre of the pilgrims, culminating with the killing of the Pope and Ursula, who is about to be slain by an archer. A warrior witnesses the scene, powerless to help; he may be the Hun prince Julio who, according to legend, had tried in vain to save the princess. On the right the funeral of the martyrs takes place in a mausoleum bearing the inscription "ursula". The veiled woman kneeling at the foot of the catafalque could be based on Orsa (Orsola), the wife of Antonio Loredan, the hero of Scutari. It is also probable that the slaughter of the pilgrims referred to the massacres of Christian men and women perpetrated by the Turks.

9. *Apotheosis of Saint Ursula*

Canvas, 481 × 335 cm
Acquisition: 1812, following the Napoleonic suppressions, (cat. 576)
Latest restoration: 1982–83

At the lower centre on the notice with the date of 1491 is written: "op. victoris/carpatio/ MCCCCLXXXXI". The alterpiece shows the apotheosis of Ursula, supported by a sheaf of palms held by a double crown of seraphs and flanked by two crossed standards. She is received in heaven by the Eternal Father who bestows the celestial crown upon her. Her companions, participants in the event, observe the scene, and to the left are three male figures who could be Giovanni, Marco and Jacopo, sons of Antonio Loredan. In the background, the walled and turreted city is evidently Cologne, while to the right on top of the mountain next to the lake is Scutari, defended against the Turks by Antonio Loredan himself. The ascension of Ursula is similar to an *Assumption of the Virgin*, and particularly to Mantegna's *Assumption* in the Ovetari chapel in Padua. For this work, as for the 1510 altarpiece for the Church of San Giobbe (Room 2, cat. 44), Carpaccio used two splendid preparatory drawings inspired by Perugino now kept in the Ashmolean Museum, Oxford.

21

9

A Neo-Classical Room

The plan of this small circular room that leads into the Albergo Room was overseen by Francesco Lazzari between 1821 and 1823, who decorated and adorned it with sculptures and bas reliefs by Canova-influenced artists.

Rinaldo Rinaldi,
Adonis, *detail*

2

3

4

6

Rinaldo Rinaldi
(Padua, 1793–Rome,
1873)

1. *Adonis*

Marble, height 153 cm
Latest restoration: 1983

On the base to the left is
the date, 1816 is
enyraved. A neo-classical
work, the *pendant* of the
statue of the same subject
in the niche in front of it.

2. *Hector Bids Farewell
to Andromache*

Bas-relief, plaster,
81 × 147 cm
Latest restoration: 1983

Rinaldi, who was a
student at the Venice
Accademia, won the
competition for
admission to the Rome
boarding house in April
1812. This bas-relief is
the trial work sent to

Venice for his second
year of study, as required
by the regulations.

3. **Antonio Giaccarelli**
(Venice, 1739–Milan,
1838)

*Priam Asks Achilles
for the Body of Hector*

Bas-relief, plaster,
96 × 180 cm
Latest restoration: 1983

Made by the artist when

he was still a student at
the Accademia between
1819 and 1825.

Jacopo De Martini
(Venice 1793-1841)

4. *Hector Scolds Paris*

Bas-relief, plaster,
90 × 180 cm
Latest restoration: 1983

De Martini won the
competition for an
apprenticeship in Rome in
1815. Due to health
problems it was difficult for
him to attend, and he
withdrew in 1818, before
completing the training.
The work was sent by him
to the Accademia during
his second year of study, as
required by the regulations.

5. *Adonis*

Marble, height: 158 cm
Latest restoration: 1983

An academic
representation of the neo-
classical standards of beauty.

6. *Enone Refuses to Assist
the Wounded Paris*

Bas relief, plaster,
90 × 156 cm

This group surmounted
the bas-relief with
Ganymede Taken by the
Eagle and is a plaster
copy made by De
Martini of the well-
known marble piece
which at that time was in
the Marciana library, and
today is in the
Archaeological Museum.

22

1

5

The former Church
of Santa Maria della Carità

The founding of the church of Santa Maria della Carità, which probably occurred at the beginning of the 12th century, is part history, part myth. According to Sansovino (1581), it was originally a small wooden building "... around a capital of an image of the Virgin, famous for various miracles." Only later was it decided to construct a church in stone on the site. In 1134 some Augustinian monks from Santa Maria in Porto relocated from Ravenna to Venice and built their convent next to the church of Santa Maria della Carità. According to legend, in 1177 Pope Alexander III – in order to escape from Ferderico Barbarossa – hid in the convent for six months and consecrated the church on April 5. From then on, every year on that date the Doge and Venetians of every class – even the inhabitants of the provinces – came to the church of Santa Maria della Carità to obtain the papal indulgence he had granted for the help received. Crossing the Grand Canal from Alexander III to the church was made easier by the construction of a bridge of boats from Campo San Vidal to Campo Santa Maria della Carità. This custom lasted until the end of the Republic. The old façade of the church can be seen in a painting kept in room 24, which illustrates the meeting of the Doge and the pope. From archival documents we know that at the end of the 13th century the church had an external portico – once very common on Venetian buildings – of which there are now only two examples remaining: one at San Giacomo di Rialto and another at San Nicolò dei Mendicoli.

Alvise Vivarini,
Enthroned Virgin with
Child and Saints, *detail*

There was also a bell tower for this original structure, which was left intact even during the modifications made in the 15th century, until on March 17, 1744, when, due to the erosion at its base, it finally succumbed and toppled into the Grand Canal. There were many illustrious figures buried there as we can deduce from the register published by Tassini in 1876; a part of this register still exists in the Seminary. The ascension of Gabriele Condulmer from the order of the Lateran Canons to the papacy (Eugene IV) in 1431, and his long pontificate, which lasted until 1447, brought new-found glory and power to the monks of La Carità. In fact, after prolonged negotiations with the members of the Scuola di Santa Maria della Carità, the monks obtained approval to enlarge the church. The new construction began in April of 1441 and was overseen by Bartolomeo Bon. Working with his son, Giovanni, Bon was responsible for all the stone work that carried the

new structure: the windows, the door with the lunette above it, the side door, the round eye which was once part of the façade, the statues of Saint Augustine, Saint Jerome and the Holy Father, the small bell-towers, the pinnacles, the leaves on the spire of the façade (most of which now lost), the side pillars, the ribs for the archivolts of the chapels, the cantilevers and every other decoration. At the same time, the walls were constructed in brick up to the roof, supported by fifteen beams of enormous dimensions from the region of Cadore, today still resting upon Bon's cantilevers which were completed in May of 1446, with the monogram "Ihesus". In 1450 the apse chapels were built and alongside Bartolomeo Bon we still find "Maestro Pantaleon", who appears to have been associated with Bon in many important workshops in Venice at that time, including the one at Ca' d'Oro. The decoration painted with large leaves which runs under the scarp wall of the roof and surrounds the eye on all the windows was the work of Ercole, the son of Jacobello del Fiore, who, in June of 1449, received fifty ducats for each work "... done in the Carità" and twelve more ducats in December of 1453 for the decoration of the chapels. Once the construction was completed, the friars decorated it with precious works of art costing a hundred ducats, which included the transport and customs expenses.
In 1453 a *Madonna* was bought from Donatello, who was sojourning in Padua at the time; the painting was placed over the door of the sacristy. Other works were commissioned from Jacopo, Gentile and Giovanni Bellini and their studio and from Cima da Conegliano. Many important funereal monuments were also erected, such as the one for the doges Marco and Agostino Barbarigo. Parts of these statues remain today and are preserved in the Franchetti Gallery at Ca' d'Oro and in the Seminary.
In 1807, the whole complex of the Carità – comprising the convent, church and school – was chosen to be the site of an Academy of Fine Arts and an accompanying gallery. Begun in 1811, the modifications were headed by the architect Giannantonio Selva. The church was completely overhauled: every decoration was removed, the "barco" (low porticoed wing) and the chapels were destroyed, the Gothic windows were walled over and the entire space was divided horizontally to create five large rooms on the upper floor, lighted by skylights for exhibiting.
The bas relief work by Bartolomeo Bon on the façade showing the coronation of the Virgin was removed, and is now preserved in the old sacristy of the church of the Salute.
From 1921 to 1923, under the direction of Gino Fogolari and with the architect Aldo Scolari, the whole space with the apses was restored including the truss ceiling and the Gothic windows on the side walls.
In 1948 the room was remodelled by Carlo Scarpa. He removed from the walls some broad replicas which were to imitate the original wall decoration, and placed the paintings on large larch panels lined with material. Out of respect to the few original architectural features remaining, the arrangement took on the appearance of a provisional exhibition space. Today the room is largely kept free to provide space for temporary shows, although some important works are on permanent display along the walls. At the end of the 19th century the remains of glass frames from the second half of the 14th century were placed on the windows of the central chapel; these frames once decorated the minor apses of the church of Santi Giovanni e Paolo.

Venetian school of the end of the 15th century

1. *Kneeling Angel with a Censer*

Saccharoidal marble, height: 100 cm

2. *Kneeling Angel with a Boat*

Saccharoidal marble, height: 104 cm

3. *Kneeling Angel with a Candlestick*

Saccharoidal marble, height: 106 cm

4. *Kneeling Angel with a Candlestick*

Saccharoidal marble, height: 98 cm

Acquisition: post 1849, (cat. S8, S9, S10, S11)

Latest restoration: 1980

These pieces reflect the influence of Pietro Lombardo, and were likely part of an altar or a grave monument. In August of 1849 the Fabbriceria di San Marco delivered them to the Archaeological Museum, from whence the Accademia received them.

1, 2, 3, 4

23

221

The Apse Triptychs
On the side walls of the apse are four triptychs that were originally in the Chiesa della Carità, on the altars of the noble chapels up against the "barco" (a structure similar to a chancel). These altars were erected between 1460 and 1464, and consecrated in 1471. Traditionally attributed to Vivarini, these triptychs were later linked to the

Bellini ambit, in particular Jacopo's studio. Records exists of drawings made in collaboration with Giovanni or rather, with Gentile and Giovanni dating the work to the late 1660's.
The archaic use of a gold background could be attributed to the use of assistants from Murano or to the wishes of the commissioners of the work. Nevertheless, the overall

form of the works, with the lunettes above, borrowed from Mantegna's altar-piece for San Zeno in Verona, must have had a great impact on Venetian artistic culture.

Jacopo Bellini, Gentile Bellini, Giovanni Bellini and collaborators

5. *Saint Lawrence between Saint John the Baptist and Saint Anthony of Paua,*

in the lunette *Madonna and Child with Angels*

Triptych
Panel, gold background
103 × 45 cm (Saints Lawrence and John the Baptist),
127 × 48 cm (Saint Anthony), 57 × 188 cm (the lunette, divided at the back into three parts)
Acquisition: 1812 (Saints Lawrence and the Baptist), following the Napoleonic suppressions, 1834 (Saint

23

5

Anthony), 1923 (the Madonna), 1954 (the two angels), from the depository of San Giovanni Evangelista from where, in 1840, they had been deposited with the Museo Correr, (cat. 621/B) Latest restoration: 2000

Originally on the altar of the chapel of Lorenzo Dolfin, dedicated to Saint Anthony of Padua and to Saint Stephen. The general arrangement appears influenced by Donatello,

especially with regard to the three saints. Giovanni's intervention is most evident in the Madonna and Saint Lawrence.

6. *Nativity and Saints Francis and Victor in the lunette Trinity between Saint Domenic and Ubaldo?* Triptych. Panels, with gold background 103 × 45 cm (Nativity),

127 × 48 cm (Saints Francis and Victor), 60 × 166 cm (lunette) Acquisition: 1834 (the saints), from the depositary of San Giovanni Evangelista, 1891 (Nativity) from Brera Collection, 1923 (the lunette), from the Correr Museum where it had been deposited, since 1840 (cat. 621) Latest restoration: 2000

This piece formed the altarpiece of the Natività chapel, belonging to Andrea Molin. The Trinity in the lunette is based on a drawing by Jacopo (British Museum, folio 56), while the manger scene appears to have been modelled after Vivarini models, such as the polyptych in Prague, or that of Conversano (cat. 581, in this room). The Virgin reveals the influence of Giovanni Bellini. On the back of *Saint Victor* are sketched some caricature profiles, probably by Giovanni.

6

**Jacopo Bellini,
Gentile Bellini,
Giovanni Bellini**
and collaborators

*7. Saint Sebastian between
Saints John the Baptist
and Saint Anthony the
Abbot, in the lunette Christ
in Pietà and two angels*

Triptych. Panels, with
gold background
103 × 45 cm (Saint
Sebastian and Saint

Anthony), 127 × 48 cm
(John the Baptist),
60 × 166 cm (lunette)

Acquisition: 1821
(Saint Sebastian and Saint
Anthony); 1834 (John
the Baptist), from the
depository of San
Giovanni Evangelista;
1927 (lunette) from the
Brera Picture Gallery
(cat. 621/A)
Latest restoration: 2000

Once the altarpiece in
chapel of San Sebastiano
by Zaccaria Vitturi. It is
an exact recomposition
of the three panels below
and they are linked
together by the
landscapes. It is held
to be the most significant
triptych. The figure of
Saint Anthony the Abbot
is a strong reminder of
the drawing by Giovanni
Bellini in the Royal

Library at Windsor,
and seems to have been
inspired by *San Prosdocimo*
by Donatello in the
Basilica of Sant'Antonio
in Padua.
Not withstanding
the persisting gold
background, the spatial
articulation of the images
and the chromatic beauty
demonstrate an awareness
of the latest in Venetian
and Paduan art.

23

7

8. *Virgin with Child and Saint Jerome and Saint Ludovic* in the lunette *Eternity and the Annunciation*

Triptych. Panels, with gold background, 127 × 48 cm (each) 59 × 170 cm (lunette)

Acquisition: 1834 (Madonna and Saints) from the depository of San Giovanni Evangelista; 1919 (lunette) with the Austrian restitutions, (cat. 621/C) Latest restoration: 2000

Originally in the chapel of Sant'Orsola which, after being sold to Andrea Molin and from him to Zuane Palestrina, belonged to Giacomo Zorzi. The missing depiction of the title saint has continued to cause perplexity among critics, but was probably due to the fact that at the first meeting with Molin, the ancona provided for five compartments, which were then reduced to only three.

23

8

9

10

12

23

11

Alvise Vivarini
(Murano 1442/43–died between 1504 and November 1505)

9. John the Baptist

Panel, 134 × 52 cm

10. Saint Mark

Panel, 133 × 51 cm
Acquisition: 1812
(cat. 618, 619)
Latest restoration: 1949

These two panels – damaged at the top – were originally in the church of San Pietro Martire on Murano. They are probably the remnants of a polyptych, and date to just after the *Madonna with Saints* (Room 23, cat. 607) of 1480. The bare landscape at the feet of the saints, particularly of John the Baptist, is particularly suggestive.

11. Nicolò di Pietro
attributed to
(documented in Venice from 1394 to 1430)

The Arrival of the Magi

Panel, 58 × 93 cm
Acquisition: 1816,
by bequest from
Girolamo Molin (cat. 12)
Latest restoration: 1995

Analysis of the work was confounded over the 19th century by the signature of Guariento, which was only called into doubt at the end of the century. The most recent restoration has brought to light the original vivid colours and exquisite elegance, and would seem to confirm the attribution of the painting to Nicolò di Pietro.

12. Nicola di Maestro Antonio di Ancona
(active from 1460 to c. 1485)

Crucifixion

Panel, 101 × 70 cm
Acquisition: 1816,
by bequest from
Girolamo Molin (cat. 51)
Latest restoration: 1995

This painting has been attributed to a long and varied series of artists, all in the Padua area, until it was recognised as an early work of the Ancona master. It probably dates to around the 1470s, given the deformation brought on by the Mantegna-inspired predella of San Zeno.

13. Gentile Bellini
(Venice 1429-1507)

The Blessed Lorenzo Giustiniani

Canvas, 221 × 155 cm
Acquisition: 1852
(cat. 570)
Undergoing restoration

On the inscription at the lower centre is the date 1455 and the signature. From the church of Madonna dell'Orto, this painting was displayed only in 1887. It may have originally been a processional standard, which would explain the poor condition of the work – the first dated piece by Gentile, painted nine years after the death of the first patriarch of Venice. Analysis of the profile of the ascetic, while further denouncing the influence of Andrea Mantegna, also reveals the artist's knack for objective painting, an ability which will eventually lead to his appointment as the official painter of the Signoria.

23

13

14

14. Bartolomeo Giolfino
(Verona c. 1410–c. 1486)

Madonna Enthroned with Child and Three Saints, and the Coronation of the Virgin with Saints

Sculpted and painted wood, 380 × 187 cm
Acquisition: 1909, by purchase (cat. S2)
Latest restoration: 2000

On the scroll on the base is the fragmentary inscription with the signature and the date of 1470. From the oratory of the Querini Palazzo in Pressano (near Verona), with the Querini coat of arms on the base itself. The work has lost much of its original colour, but the engraving work – also fragmentary – is a highly refined example of a Gothic style.

15. Maestro della Madonna del Parto

The Madonna del Parto and Two Devotees

Panel, 188 × 138 cm
Acquisition: 1916 (cat. 1328)
Latest restoration: 1996

On the open book is an invocation to the Virgin Mary, Madonna del Parto.

23

16

The work is from the late 14th century and comes from the church of Santa Caterina. Similar to other early works by Nicolò di Pietro, this work was probably painted in Venice, although it was previously attributed to an Emilian artist.

16. **Bartolomeo Vivarini** (Venice c. 1430-records up until 1491)

Madonna Enthroned

Panels, gold background, 131 × 49, 107 × 33 cm, Acquisition: 1812 (cat. 615)
Latest restoration: 1994

In the centre compartment toward the bottom is the signature and date of 1454. The polyptych comes from the church of S. Andrea on the island of Certosa, where it was placed at the altar of the Ca' Morosini chapel. An engraving by G. Sasso provides testimony of the now lost frame with a *Crucifixion*

engraved among the half-figures of prophets. This is one of the most important works by the artist; the *Virgin with Child* will be alluded to by Giovanni Bellini in his *Madonna Enthroned* (Room 4, cat. 591).

23

15

17

18

20

21

Alvise Vivarini
(Murano 1442/43–died
between 1504 and
November 1505)

17. *Beatified Martyr*
Panel, 143 × 40 cm
Acquisition: 1919, with
the Austrian restitutions,
(cat. 593/A)

18. *Saint Claire*
Panel, 144 × 38 cm
Acquisition: 1828,
following the Napoleonic
suppressions, (cat. 593)
Latest restoration: 1948
Recorded by Boschini
(1664) in the church of San
Daniele, originally used by

Benedictine nuns, and from
1437 by Augustinian nuns.
Chiara Ogniben Sustan was
responsible for the change
of order; the
psychologically charged
face of Saint Claire (Chiara)
has led some critics to
suggest that this may be a

portrait of Chiara Ogniben
Sustan. The position of the
green curtains on the two
panels implies that they
were two independent
works and not part of a
larger piece. The works date
from 1485-1490.

19. *Madonna Enthroned*
Panel, 175 × 196 cm
Acquisition: 1812,
following the Napoleonic
suppressions, (cat. 607)
Latest restoration: 1993

On the base of the throne is
the date 1480 and the
signature. The work was
originally on the altar of
Santa Maria della Prà, and
then on the altar of San
Bernardino in the church of
San Francesco in Treviso,
which the minor friars
beautified with works by
Venetian artists – including
Giovanni Mansueti and
Carpaccio – over the 15th
and 16th centuries
(Quadreria cat. 97 and 90).
The work is a masterpiece:
the green curtain behind,
while still quite old, was
added at a later date and is
of a material that x-ray
analyses have not been able
to penetrate. The
composition must have
originally been arranged

23

19

with the windows opening on to the landscape, as in the *Virgin Adoring the Sleeping Baby Jesus* in the church of San Giovanni in Bragora. The bust of Saint Anthony also appears on a panel in the Museo Correr.

Bartolomeo Vivarini
(c. 1430–records until 1491)

20. Saint Mary Magdalene

Panel, 132 × 48 cm

21. Saint Barbara

Panel, 132 × 48 cm
Acquisition: 1812,
following the Napoleonic
suppressions, (cat. 584, 585)
Latest restoration: 1979

The signature and date (1490) appear on the scroll on the lower part of Saint Barbara. These two works come from the now destroyed church of San Geminiano in Venice. They are from the later period of the artist's life, and present a monumentality that foreshadows the next century.

22. Saint Ambrose Blessing the Devotees, with Saints Louis, Peter, Paul and Sebastian

Panel, gold background,
125 × 47 cm (central),
108 × 36 cm (sides)
Acquisition: 1919, with the
Austrian restitutions, (cat. 825)
Latest restoration: 1997

On the lower part of Saint Peter are the signature and date (1477); on the lower part of Saint Paul is the

23

signature of the creator of the lost frame: Giacomo da Faenza. This polyptych comes from the Tagliapietra Confraternity, and was probably a devotional piece donated by some members and dedicated to their personal saints, as the writing under Saint Ambrose would indicate. The work has a surprisingly impressionist effect, with a similarly strong use of colour.

23. **Lazzaro Bastiani**
(Venice, 1425/30–c. 1512)

Nativity Scene with Saints James, Eustacius, Nicholas and Mark

Panel, 160 × 191 cm
Acquisition: 1812,
following the Napoleonic
suppressions, (cat. 100)
Latest restoration: 1994

Originally in the church of Sant'Elena. The painting was completed according to the

will of Eustachio Balbi, who died in 1480. The design of the dwelling seems inspired by similar dwellings painted by Jacopo Bellini in the books of drawings in the Louvre and the British Museum. The unusual format of the piece is similar to the *Virgin and Saints* by Alvise Vivarini (Room 23, cat. 607), dating from 1480. The artist's illusionistic ability to create extreme depth through the structure of the dwelling is impressive.

22a   22b   22c   22d   22e

24. **Andrea da Murano**
(records from 1463 to 1504)

Saints Vincent Ferreri and Roch, with Saint Sebastian and Saint Peter the Martyr, Madonna della Misericordia with Saints Louis (?), Dominic, Thomas Aquinas and Catherine of Siena

Canvas transferred from a panel, 152 × 88 cm (central panel); panel, 152 × 47 cm (sides); panel, 80 × 199 cm (lunette)
Acquisition: the pieces of the work, which was returned after the Napoleonic suppressions, were united in 1883, (cat. 28)
Latest restoration: 1948

Signed at the lower centre, this triptych was originally in the church of San Pietro Martire on Murano. All of the saints represented on the lower order – including Saint Peter, after whom the church was named – are venerated for their magical qualities against the plague; Saint Roch indicates a bubo under his clothing, while the small devotees and commissioners kneeling seem to be praying for protection against contagion. The artist was an attentive observer of the artistic trends developing in those years in the area of the Venetian lagoon, and was among the few Venetians who truly understood the work of Andrea del Castagno. The work was surely painted in relation to a plague, probably the one of 1478.

Carlo Crivelli
(Venice 1430/35–died between August 7, 1494, and September, 1495)

25. *Saints Peter and Paul*

Panel, 218 × 54 cm

26. *Saints Jerome and Augustine*

Panel, 187 × 72 cm

25   26

Acquisition: 1883 (Saints Jerome and Augustine); 1895 (Saints Peter and Paul) by purchase (cat. 103, 103/A)

Latest restoration: 1979

Originally in the Cathedral of Camerino, where they were located alongside the *Madonna della Candeletta*. The church was destroyed by an earthquake in 1799, and the *Madonna* and *Saints Jerome and Augustine* were taken to the Brera gallery in Milan; they were transferred to the Accademia in 1883. The panel with *Saint Peter and Paul* was recovered from under the rubble and sold to the State. In spite of the fact that the expressionism of the saints seems to be in contrast with the formal elegance of the Madonna, the pieces were part of a single complex, as is shown by the similar dimensions and the repetition of the identical parapet. As the central panel is signed with the title of *eques*, an honour bestowed upon the painter in 1490 by prince Ferdinando of Capua, the paintings should correspond to around that date.

27. **Bartolomeo Vivarini and workshop**
(c. 1430-records until 1491)

Conversano Polyptych

Panels, 154 × 46 cm (central), 138 × 23 cm (sides), 25 × 270 cm (predella), 46 × 45 cm (cyma)

Acquisition: 1883, by purchase from the Conversano duomo, (cat. 581)

Latest restoration: 1995

On the central panel is shown the Nativity scene, with Saints Francis, Andrew, John the Baptist, Peter, Paul, Jerome, Dominic and Theodore. Below in the Nativity scene is an inscription with the date (1475), while on the listel of the predella frame is another with the signature. The fact that the work was to be sent to Apulia made it a less binding undertaking for the artist. Although the central group translates the one made by Antonio Vivarini for a 1447 polyptych into more substantial and animated forms, the saints at the sides and the predella seem weaker and not to have been painted by the artist himself.

23

27

Canvases from the Sala dell'Albergo of the Scuola Grande di San Marco.

The five canvases located at the back of the church, together with the *Sermon of Saint Mark at Alexandria* by Gentile Bellini and the *Baptism of Saint Mark* by Giovanni Mansueti – today in the Brera Museum – were part of the original decoration of the Albergo Room of the Scuola di San Marco. In 1492 Gentile and Giovanni Bellini offered to paint the room, and came to an agreement with the Scuola. However, Gentile died in 1507 without finishing the *Sermon*, which was completed by Giovanni. In 1515 the Scuola hired Giovanni to paint the *Martyrdom of Saint Mark*, but unfortunately on November 29, 1516, the artist died and the work was left unfinished until Vittore Belliniano completed it in 1526. Later works were commissioned from Giovanni Mansueti, collaborator and disciple of Gentile Bellini, thus guaranteeing the stylistic continuity of the cycle. Mansueti died in 1526 or 1527, and the last two paintings, *The Presentation of Saint Mark's Ring* by Paris Bordon, and the *Sea Storm (Burrasca di mare)* by Palma il Vecchio, reveal a radical change in the taste of the commissioners. When the Scuola was suppressed by Napoleonic decree in 1806, the cycle was dispersed, with pieces in Milan, Venice and Vienna. The works in Vienna were returned in 1919 and the cycle was re-assembled at the Accademia Galleries in 1994 (but without the paintings in the Brera Museum).

2

1. Giovanni Bellini
(1434/39-1516) and
Vittore Belliniano
(records from 1507 to 1529)

Martyrdom of Saint Mark

Canvas, 362 × 771 cm,
the central cut at door
level is 158 × 172 cm
Acquisition: 1919, with
the Austrian restitutions,
(cat. 1002)
Latest restoration: 1987-94

On July 4th, 1515, the
Scuola commissioned
Giovanni Bellini to paint
a canvas with the story of
Saint Mark, who "... in
Alexandria was dragged
along the ground by
those infidel Moors".
This is the scene of the
martyrdom that appears
in the Marciani mosaics:
during the Easter feast
Mark's adversaries had
sent soldiers to arrest the
saint; dragging him by a
cord tied around his neck
they went through the
streets of Alexandria for
the entire day and until
the next morning when

he died. The paintings in
the Doge's Palace have
been lost, so this is one of
the very rare examples of
the artist's larger
decorative works,
although it was not
painted entirely by him.
In fact, when Giovanni
died on November 19,
1516, the work was
completed by Vittore
Belliniano, Bellini's co-
worker in the Doge's
Palace, who placed his
signature on it and the
date of 1526; ten years
later. The drawing and
preparation of the great
canvas are doubtless the
work of Giovanni based
on a sketch by his
brother, but the actual
painting on the canvas
was by Vittore. Perhaps, as
recent critics have
proposed, he also had the
collaboration of Lorenzo
Lotto, who was a guest of
the convent of Santi
Giovanni e Paolo,
attached to the Scuola di
San Marco, from 1525 to

1526. But it is clear that
Bellini was responsible
for the view with San
Ciriaco of Ancona in the
background on the hill,
which is similar to the
one that appears on
Nicolini's *Crucifixion*
which is now in Prato.

2. Giovanni Mansueti
(records from 1485–died
between September,
1526, and March, 1527)

Saint Mark Heals Aniano

Canvas, 370 × 407 cm
Acquisition: 1838 (cat. 569)
Latest restoration. 1992-94

This painting and the
Baptism of Aniano, today
in the Brera Gallery,
surely refer to the "doi
telleri in albergo" (the
two canvases in the Sala
dell'Albergo) that the
Scuola decided to have
painted on October 24,
1518. Gentile Bellini died
in 1507, Giovanni in
1516, and Vittore
Belliniano was still
occupied on his

Martyrdom so Mansueti, a
disciple primarily of
Gentile, whose drawings
he had worked on, with
his somewhat behind-
the-times taste must have
seemed a logical choice
to guarantee the stylistic
unity of the cycle. The
Guardian Grande
Antonio de Maistri
commissioned the piece,
assigning the third canvas
to Mansueti in 1525,
presumably the year
when the two paintings
were completed. This
painting was to left
(Room 23, cat. 516), after
the *Sea-Storm* and the
*Presentation of Saint Marks
Ring* (Room 23, cat.
320). It depicts an
episode in the life of
Saint Mark. When he
reache Alexandria, he
breaks a strap on his
sandal and the archangel
Michael appears to him
and has Mark follow him
so he can show Mark his
successor. Mark finds the
cobbler Aniano and gives
the sandal to him. While
Aniano is repairing the
sandal, he injures his left
hand, which Mark heals
with his saliva mixed
with dust from the street.
The scene takes place
within an interesting
architectural context; the
building at the back with
the veiled women recalls
the *Prayer*, now in the
Brera gallery, and the
descriptions of Vasari of a
lost painting by Alvise
Vivarini in the Sala del
Maggior Consiglio; the
decorations of this Sala
were the inspiration for
the entire cycle in the
Albergo. An inscription at
the centre describes the
miracle, while to the
lower left a camel driver
holds a scroll with the
artist's signature.

1

3. **Giovanni Mansueti**
(records from 1485–died
between September, 1526
and March, 1527)

*Episodes from the Life of
Saint Mark*

Canvas, 371 × 603 cm
Acquisition: 1838,
following the Napoleonic
suppressions, (cat. 562)
Latest restoration: 1992-94

To the lower left, a baby
holds a scroll with the
artist's signature. This work
was originally in the Sala
dell'Albergo between the
two windows, and was
commissioned by the
Guardian Grande Antonio
di Maistri in 1525. When
Mansueti was dying,
between September 1526
and March 1527, the
painting was nearly
finished, although "some
heads" had not yet been
added. The composition is
articulated in three

episodes. To the right, under a loggia, the idolatrous Egyptians plot against Mark, envious of his ever-growing number of followers. At the centre, the saint is beset by enemies while celebrating mass and they then drag him through the streets of Alexandria. To the left, he is brought into jail, where an angel appears to him to announce his entrance into a new life. At this announcement Mark thanks Jesus and prays for him to receive his soul, at which point Jesus appears to him and speaks the famous words "Pax tibi, Marce, evangelista meus" ("Peace be with you, Mark, my Evangelist"). According to the affirmations of his daughter Cecilia, Mansueti included the portraits of the more important members of the Scuola in the painting.

3

4. Jacopo Palma il Vecchio
(Serina, Bergamo, c. 1480–Venice 1528) and
Paris Bordon
(Treviso 1500–Venice 1571)

Sea Storm

Canvas, 362 × 408 cm
Acquisition: 1829,
following the Napoleonic
suppressions, (cat. 516)
Latest restoration: 1993–94

This work was originally in the Sala dell'Albergo, immediately to the left after entering. The work was almost certainly referred to by the Scuola on November 5, 1534, when the room was described as decorated "with paintings", including "the painting that will be delivered in a few days". It must have remained unfinished or in some way damaged after its completion, as the large insert to the right with the boat containing the fisherman and the three saints would attest; this part has been attributed to Paris Bordon. Before displaying it at the Accademia Galleries in 1830, the part to the lower left with the John Dory was also added by Sebastiano Santi in order to fill in the missing part corresponding to a doorway. This painting and the following one depict the legend of a terrible storm with very high seas that occurred on the night of February 25, 1341. An old fisherman found shelter under a bridge in the place that was then called Terranova, where the public granaries were located and where the formerly royal gardens are now. A man came to the fisherman from the nearby church of San Marco, and asked the fisherman to take him to the island of San Giorgio, where another stranger also boarded the boat. They then went towards San Nicolò del Lido, where a third person came aboard. While the storm raged on, Saint Mark, Saint George and Saint Nicholas all appeared to the fisherman. Suddenly a large galley containing countless devils appeared in the churning sea before them and headed towards Venice to destroy the city. The three angels intervened and sent the ship to the bottom of the sea. Before returning into his church as the other saints had done, Mark gave the astonished fisherman a ring to give to the Doge as proof of the events he had witnessed.

The sailboat at the centre was inspired by a drawing by Lorenzo Lotto for one of the inlaid wood pieces of Santa Maria Maggiore in Bergamo. The authorship of the painting, whose identification was always problematic, has been

4

made difficult by the many changes and additions made to the piece. In 1550 Vasari attributed it to Giorgione, but in the 1568 edition he attributed it to Palma. It is probable that after the death of Mansueti between 1527 and 1528, the painting was indeed entrusted to Palma, who was a member of the Scuola from 1513 until his death on July 30, 1528. The work was probably commissioned in the years immediately prior to this date, and so he may not have had the time to finish the canvas, which instead was completed or repaired by Paris Bordon in 1534.

5. **Paris Bordon**
(Treviso 1500–Venice 1571)
Presentation of Saint Mark's Ring
Canvas by transposition from another canvas, 370 × 300 cm
Acquisition: 1815, following the Napoleonic suppressions, with the restitutions from Paris, (cat. 320)
Latest restoration: 1988

This work was originally in the Sala dell'Albergo, on the left between *Sea Storm* and *Saint Mark Heals Aniano*. The work is related to the Scuola's decision on January 12, 1534 to have made "uno o doi teleri" ("one or two paintings"), for which a competition was

held. On the base of the pillar at right is the signature. The work shows the fisherman who offers the ring of Saint Mark – which tradition still holds as being among the treasures of the Basilica – to the Doge as proof of the miraculous events of the night before. Surrounding Doge Andrea Gritti (1522-38) are the senators, while on the left is the Great Guardian and a group of members of the confraternity. The complex architectural setting of the background – suggestive of the Doge's Palace – was inspired by Sebastiano Serlio. The decision of 1534 notwithstanding, this

painting, which was enthusiastically praised by Vasari, dates to the early 1540s, as is evidenced by its adhesion to the teachings of Titian and of the Tuscan artists in Venice at that time.

23

5

The former Sala dell'Albergo
of the Scuola di Santa Maria della Carità

This was the Albergo Room of the Scuola di Santa Maria della Carità, where the most highly ranked members met, and where the registers, charters (called the "mariegola"), and the relics were all kept. The ceiling, gilt and multicoloured, with the four *Evangelists*, dates from the end of the 15th century. The *Holy Father* at the centre was probably taken from a previous ceiling in the Assembly Hall which may have been destroyed by fire. In 1811 Selva opened the short stairway; for this occasion the wooden altar was disassembled and the triptych by Antonio Vivarini and Giovanni d'Alemagna was moved to the right wall.

Tiziano Vecellio, called Titian
Presentation of Mary
in the Temple, *detail*

1. **Antonio Vivarini**
(c. 1418/20–1476/84)
Giovanni d'Alemagna
(records from 1441–50)

The Virgin Enthroned with Saints Gregory, Jerome, Ambrose and Augustine

Canvases
344 × 203 cm (central),
344 × 137 cm (sides)
Acquisition: 1807
(cat. 625)
Latest restoration: 1999

On the step of the throne is written the date 1446 and the signature. This work was painted for the Albergo Room, for the wall in front of Titian's *Presentation of Mary in the Temple* (cat. 626), where the inserted wooden frame was destroyed along with the altar in 1811, when the connecting access was opened. One of the oldest Venetian paintings on canvas, it is certainly the most unified work the two artists produced in their problematic collaboration. The Virgin and angels are clearly attributable to Vivarini. The new notions about perspective are evident in spite of the abundance of decoration, which must have appeared even more opulent when completed with the original frames. These notions probably reflect the artists' awareness of the graphic studies Donatello made in preparation for the Santo altar in Padua.

24

1

2. **Tiziano Vecellio, called 'Titian'**
(Pieve di Cadore
c. 1480/90-Venice 1576)

Presentation of the Virgin

Canvas, 335 × 775 cm
Acquisition: 1807
(cat. 626)
Latest restoration: 1981

This large canvas was painted for the Albergo Room of the Scuola della Carità between August 21, 1534 and March 6, 1539. In addition to this subject, the walls of the room were also decorated to the left by the *Marriage of the Virgin* by Giampietro Silvio, and to the right by Girolamo Dente's *Annunciation*, still in storage at the parish of Mason Vicentino and now in the storerooms of the museum.
The painting appears to have been cut below to accommodate the two doors. The door to the observer's right already existed and was probably the Gothic doorway, today walled over, which was the old entrance of the ground floor room. The left door was opened on March 10, 1527, while Titian was still alive, and required the sacrifice of part of the painting. Although the horizontal path of the wall incorporates a certain design taken from the Venetian narrative tradition – and mostly from Carpaccio – it does so with an extraordinarily "modern" spirit and a deep awareness of the contemporary architectural notions proposed by Sansovino and Serlio. The perfect balance between architecture and landscape, and of both together with the open procession of the members of the confraternity, firmly establishes the unity of the work, a new interpretation of the 15th century models and of great importance for the painters who followed.

24

2

3

4

24

3. Veneto–Byzantine School of the 14th and 15th Centuries

Reliquary of Cardinal Bessarione

Wood, silver, gilt filigree, enamel, glass and precious stones, 47 × 32 cm
Acquisition: 1919, with the suppression of the Scuola, it first entered the collection of Luigi Savorgnan and later that of Abbot Luigi Celotti, who sold it to the Emperor Francis I in 1821. Assigned to the Galleries with the Austrian restitutions, (cat. S19)

Donated to the Scuola della Carità in 1463 by Cardinal Bessarione, the famous scholar who with the bequest of his manuscripts brought about the institution of the Marciana library. This piece, which even Gentile Bellini helped to construct, was originally located in a tabernacle (now dispersed) on the altar on the wall where now the short stairway begins. The precious piece is formed of a cross with Christ encased on an enamelled tablet which includes four rock crystal cases containing the "Holy Wood" and "Holy Shroud" relics, two plates with the archangels Gabriel and Michael, Constantine and Saint Helena painted on glass, a cover composed of a fixed part framing the reliquary on three sides with seven small scenes from *The Passion* and a moveable shutter cover on which the Crucifixion is depicted. The origin and date of the rare and complex work is problematic, not only because of the difficulty of interpreting the Greek and Latin inscriptions, but also because the embedding for the cross and the painted cover are probably the work of Bessarione.

4. Anonymous 16th century Veneto artist

Portrait of Cardinal Bessarione

Canvas, 116 × 95 cm
Acquisition: 1807, following the Napoleonic suppressions, (cat. 876)

Originally in the Sala dell'Albergo, this painting was commissioned by the Scuola della Carità on March 8, 1540. Cardinal Bessarione is depicted holding the reliquary given to him by the Scuola itself and wearing the apparel of a member of the confraternity.

5. Venetian School 16th Century

Doge Ziani Meets Pope Alexander III at the Chiesa della Carità

Canvas, 185 × 234 cm
Acquisition: 1884, from the Doge's Palace, (cat. 654)

This painting may originally have been in the Carità church. It depicts Doge Ziani meeting Pope Alexander III. According to legend, the pope had come to Venice while fleeing Barbarossa. The piece is also interesting for documentary reasons, as it shows how the façade of the church and the Scuola appeared in the 16th century.

24

5

The "Quadreria" Gallery

In the early seventies on the top floor of the Palladian Monastery, the Accademia Galleries were provided with a repository created with two aims in mind: a secondary gallery in the long corridor, well in keeping with the existing building, and a room for consultation in a spacious enclosed environment, with the paintings arranged on fixed metal trellises. The long, elegant corridor was conceived by Andrea Palladio as an entranceway to the cells of the large religious order, the Lateran canons for whom he had "tried to make this abode like that of the Ancients'". Access to it is afforded from the oval stairway of which the architect himself wrote: "I made of it an empty place in the middle of the *Monastero della Carità* in Venice that is truly admirable". Indeed, as he had predicted in his treatise, "when standing atop the stairway, one can see – and be seen by – everyone who ascends or begins to ascend".

These structural works belonging now to the distant past, both the stairway and corridor were in need of full restoration, and the paintings required a more fitting position. By fortuitous coincidence, the restoration works of 1995 were undertaken at almost the same time as the restoration of the terracotta façade, dated 1561, and of the *tablinum*, which in the house of the ancients was the space dedicated to the Penates or household gods and used as a vestry, and which today belongs to the Academy of Fine Arts.

The long corridor has been conceived as a type of storeroom, which is organised chronologically with suitable lighting and fittings. Here, about 80 paintings are found and can be viewed not just by scholars but also by all visitors, upon prior booking.

Nicolò di Pietro
(recorded in Venice from 1394
to 1430)
*The Virgin with Child with Saint
Martha and Saint Catherine*
canvas, 104 × 139 cm
Acquisition: 1960, from the state
depository (cat. 1237)
Latest restoration: 1995

**Marco Antonio di Ruggero
known as 'Marco Zoppo'**
(Cento 1453 – Venice 1478)
Master of the Cattaver
(active in Venice between 1460
and c. 1470)
*Christ Blessing with Saints Vincent
Ferrer, Augustine, Helen and Francis*
Canvas, 136 × 407 cm
Acquisition: 1838, following
the Napoleonic suppressions,
(cat. 614, 622, 620)
Latest restoration: 1984-87

Lazzaro Bastiani
(Venice c. 1425/30-1512)
Saint Anthony in the Nut-Tree
Arched panel, 234 × 140 cm
Acquisition: 1862, following the
Napoleonic suppression (cat. 104)
Saint Veneranda Enthroned
Arched panel, 325 × 217 cm
Acquisition: 1919, with the
Austrian restitutions (cat. 822)
Latest restoration: 1995

**Gerolamo da Treviso
il Vecchio**
(Gerolamo di Bartolomeo
Strazzaroli di Aviano, 1451-97)
*The Virgin Enthroned with
a Franciscan Bishop (Louis?)
and Saints Anthony, Francis
and Prosdocimo (or Basil)*
Panel, 208 × 214 cm
Acquisition: 1915-18,
spoils of war (cat. 886)
Latest restoration: 1995

The Transfiguration
Panel in the shape of a lunette,
172 × 263 cm
Acquisition: 1812, following the
Napoleonic suppressions (cat. 96)

Pier Maria Pennacchi
(Treviso 1464-1514/15)
Death of the Virgin
Panel, 134 × 168 cm
Acquisition: 1907, by purchase
(cat. 657)
Latest restoration: 1995

**Giovanni Buonconsiglio,
known as 'Marescalco'**
(Montecchio Maggiore, Vicenza?
c. 1465 – died 1536/37)
*Saint Benedict, Saint Thecla
and Saint Damian*
Panel, 82 × 68 cm
Acquisition: 1856, by purchase
the Manfrin Collection (cat. 602)
Latest restoration: 1958

Nicolò Rondinelli
(recorded from 1495 to 1502)
*The Virgin and Child with Saint
Jerome*
Panel, 82 × 59 cm
Acquisition: 1917, by purchase
(cat. 904)
Latest restoration: 1995

Giovanni Mansueti
(records from 1485 – died
between September 1526
and March 1527)
*Saint Sebastian with Saints Liberale,
Gregory, Francis and Roch*
Panel, 203 × 201 cm
Acquisition: 1810, following the
Napoleonic suppressions (cat. 97)
Latest restoration: 1995

Giovanni Agostino da Lodi
(active 1590s, with records up
to c. 1520)
*Virgin and Child with Saints Simon
and Saint Jerome*
Panel, 71 × 111 cm
Acquisition: 1838, following
the Napoleonic suppressions,
(cat. 605)
Latest restoration: 1990

Francesco Morone
(Verona 1471-1529)
The Virgin and Child
Canvas, 72 × 54 cm
Acquisition: 1932, by purchase
from Giovannelli collecton,
(cat. 916)

**Bartolomeo Cincani,
known as Montagna**
(Vicenza c. 1449 – 11 October,
1523)
*The Virgin and Child Enthroned
with Saint Sebastian and Saint
Jerome*
Panel, 215 × 162 cm
Acquisition: 1816, bequest
of Girolamo Molin (cat. 80)
Latest restoration: 1994-95

**Giambattista Cima
da Conegliano**
(Conegliano 1459-1517)
*The Archangel Raphael
and Tobias with Saint Nicholas
and Saint James the Great*
Canvas transferred from panel,
162 × 178 cm
Acquisition: 1888, by purchase
(cat. 592)

**Giambattista Cima da
Conegliano**, workshop of
(Conegliano 1459-1517)
*Saint Mark Enthroned with Saint
Andrew and Saint Louis*
Canvas, 222 × 341 cm (cat. 816)
Justice
Canvas, 189 × 80 cm (cat. 165)
Temperance
Canvas, 189 × 85 cm (cat. 167)
Acquisition: 1838, the two lateral
figures following the Napoleonic
suppressions; 1919, the central
section with the Austrian
restitutions
Latest restoration: 1959

Vittore Carpaccio
(Venice? c. 1460 – before 1525)
*Meeting of Joachim and Anne, with
Saint Louis IX and Saint Libera*
Panel, 186 × 169 cm
Acquisition: 1812, following the
Napoleonic suppressions (cat. 90)
Latest restoration: 1995

Francesco Bissolo
(c. 1475-1554)
*The Presentation of Christ to Simeon
with Saints and the Donor*
Panel, 80 × 119 cm
Acquisition: 1950, bequest
of Felicita Renier (cat. 93)
Latest restoration: 1995

Lorenzo Luzzo
(documented from 1511 to 1526)
*The Virgin and Child with Saint
Vitus, Saint Modesto and Christ
the Redeemer in Glory*
Canvas, 187 × 120 cm
Acquisition: 1926, by purchase
(cat. 814)
Latest restoration: 1988

Marco Basaiti
(Venice 1470/75–post 1530)

Saint George and the Princess

Canvas, 229 × 156 cm
Acquisition: 1899, by purchase,
(cat. 102)
Latest restoration: 1994

Marco Basaiti?
(Venice 1470/75–post 1530)

Portrait of a Man

Panel, 31 × 23 cm
Acquisition: 1900 by purchase
(cat. 645)
Latest restoration: 1995

Veneto School of the Second decade of the 16th century

Christ with the Doctors

Panel, 152 × 176 cm
Acquisition: 1816, bequest of
Girolamo Molin, (cat. 85)
Latest restoration: 1995

Benedetto Rusconi, known as 'Diana'
(Venice c. 1460-1525)

The Virgin and Child with Saints Jerome, Benedict, Mary Magdalene and Justina

Panel, 200 × 230 cm
Acquisition: 1812, following the
Napoleonic suppressions, (cat. 82)
Latest restoration: 1995

Giovanni Francesco Caroto
(Verona c. 1480-1555)

The Madonna Sewing

Canvas, 59 × 47 cm
Acquisition: 1889, by purchase,
(cat. 609)
Latest restoration: 1995

Rocco Marconi
(Treviso c. 1470/75–recorded in
Venice from 1504, died before 13
May, 1529)

Christ with Saint John the Baptist and Saint Peter

Canvas, 185 × 124 cm
Acquisition: 1812, following the
Napoleonic suppressions (cat. 317)
Latest restoration: 1957-58

Sebastiano Florigerio
(Conegliano? c. 1500/05–died after
1550 and before December 29,
1564)

The Virgin and Child with Saint Anne

between Saint Roch and Saint Sebastian (in the lunette)
Saint John the Evangelist with Saint Anthony of Padua and Saint Francis
also called *The Immaculate Conception Altarpiece*

Panel, 240 × 181 cm (lower
section), 94 × 185 cm (lunette)
Acquisition: 1829, following the
Napoleonic suppressions, (cat. 157)
Latest restoration: 1995

Jacopo Negretti known as Palma il Vecchio and workshop
(Serina, Bergamo c. 1480-Venice
1528)

Christ and the Woman of Canaan

Panel, 95 × 155 cm
Acquisition: 1838, donated by
Girolamo Contarini, (cat.310)
Latest restoration: 1995

Titian and workshop
(c. 1480/90-1576)

Symbol of Saint Luke (Bull)

Panel, 455 × 2360 cm (cat.1035a)

Symbol of Saint Matthew (Angel)

Panel, 495 × 2030 cm (cat. 1035b)

Symbol of Saint Mark (Lion)

Panel, 455 × 2400 cm (cat. 1035c)

Symbol of Saint John (Eagle)

Panel, 495 × 1980 cm (cat. 1035d)

Cherub Head

Panel, 45 × 40 cm (cat. 1035m)

Two Cherub Heads

Panel, 40,5 × 46,5 cm (cat. 1035t)

Mask of Satyr

Panel, 59 × 58 cm (cat. 1035h)

Face of a Woman

Panel, 49 × 43 cm (cat.1035o)
Acquisition: 1812, following the
Napoleonic suppressions
Latest restoration: 1989

Paris Bordon
(Treviso 1500-Venice 1571)

Winged Putti with Garlands

Panel, 52 × 101 cm
Acquisition: 1816,
donated by Girolamo Molin, (cat. 311)
Latest restoration: 1980

Bonifacio de' Pitati known as Bonifacio Veronese
(Verona 1487-Venice 1553)

Christ and the Apostles

Panel, 189 × 151 cm
Acquisition: 1814, following the
Napoleonic suppressions, (cat. 309)
Latest restoration: 1955

The Visiting Angel

Canvas, 198 × 135 cm
Acquisition: 1919, with the
Austrian restitutions, (cat. 942)

The Virgin

Canvas, 197 × 137 cm
Acquisition: 1919, with the
Austrian restitutions, (cat. 943)
Latest restoration: 1963

Andrea Meldolla, known as Schiavone
(Zadar c. 1510/15-Venice 1563)

Christ before Pilate

Canvas, 104 × 170 cm
Acquisition: 1850, bequest
of Felicita Renier, (cat. 271)
Latest restoration: 1956

Jacopo Robusti, known as Tintoretto
(Venice 1519-1594)

The Crucifixions on Mount Ararat

Incomplete panel, 138 × 218 cm
Acquisition: 1865, following the
Napoleonic suppressions, (cat. 1091)
Latest restoration: 1960

Saint Peter

Canvas, 104 × 33 cm
Acquisition: 1838, donated by
Girolamo Contarini, (cat. 506)
Latest restoration: 1960

Saint Paul

Canvas, 104 × 33 cm
Acquisition: 1838, donated by
Girolamo Contarini, (cat. 501)
Latest restoration: 1960

The Presentation of Christ at the Temple

Canvas, 237 × 296 cm
Acquisition: 1960, by decree, (cat. 725)
Latest restoration: 1986

The Deposition

Canvas, 227 × 294 cm
Acquisition: 1806, following the
Napoleonic suppressions, (cat. 217)
Latest restoration: 1989

Jacopo dal Ponte, known as Bassano, workshop of
(Bassano c. 1510-1594)

Adoration of the Shepherds

Canvas, 120 × 222 cm
Acquisition: 1933, from the State
depository, (cat. 902)
Latest restoration: 1956

Jacopo dal Ponte, known as Bassano and assistants
(Bassano c. 1510-1594)

The Virgin and Child Enthroned in Glory with Saint Jerome

Canvas, 220 × 161 cm
Acquisition: 1930, from the state depository, (cat. 920)

Paolo Caliari, known as Veronese
(Verona 1528-1588)

Assumption of the Virgin

Canvas, 396 × 200 cm
Acquisition: 1812, following the Napoleonic suppressions, (cat. 265)
Latest restoration: 1988

Paolo Caliari, known as Veronese, workshop of
(Verona 1528-1588)

The Madonna of the Rosary

Canvas, 173 × 316 cm
Acquisition: 1844, following the Napoleonic suppressions, (cat. 207)
Latest restoration: 1986-87

Carlo Caliari
(Venice 1570-1596)

Saint Augustine Dictating his Rules to the Lateran Canons

Canvas, 285 × 146 cm
Acquisition: 1919, with the Austrian restitutions, (cat. 813)

Domenico Robusti, known as Domenico Tintoretto
(Venice 1560-1635)

Two Portraits of Confreres from the Scuola dei Mercanti

Canvas, 330 × 194 cm each
Acquisition: 1919, with the Austrian restitutions, (cat. 872, 873)
Latest restoration: 1956

Anonymous Veneto artist
(early 17th century)

Young Woman playing the Guitar and Onlooker

Detached fresco, 107 × 122 cm

An Old Man and a Young Woman

Detached fresco, 106 × 122 cm
Acquisition: 1827, following its removal prior to the demolition of the building which housed it, (cat. 731, 733)
Latest restoration: 1995

Jacopo Negretti, known as Palma il Giovane
(Venice 1548-1628)

Susanna and the Old Men

Canvas, 96 × 79 cm
Acquisition: 1838, donated by Girolamo Molin, (cat. 538)
Latest restoration: 1955

The Pleasures of the Prodigal Son
Canvas, 83 × 118 cm
Acquisition: 1838, donated by Girolamo Molin, (cat. 634)
Latest restoration: 1958

Return of the Prodigal Son
Canvas, 83 × 118 cm
Acquisition: 1838, donated by Girolamo Molin, (cat. 684)
Latest restauration: 1958

The Dead Christ, Held by Three Angels
Canvas, 130 × 108 cm
Acquisition: 1850, bequest of Felicita Renier, (cat. 267)
Latest restoration: 1994

Alessandro Varotari, known as Padovanino
(Padua 1590-Venice 1650)

Frieze with Putti
Canvas, 495 × 97 cm
Acquisition: 1835, from the state depository, (cat. 802)
Latest restoration: 1962

Orpheus and Eurydice
Canvas, 164 × 119 cm
Acquisition: donated by Girolamo Contarini, (cat. 548)
Latest restoration: 1994

Francesco Maffei
(Vicenza c. 1605-Padua 1660)

The Virgin Appears to Saint Filippo Neri
Canvas, 215 × 145 cm
Acquisition: 1838, 1865 from the state depository, (cat. 1093)
Latest restoration: 1961

Charles Le Brun
(Paris 1619-1690)

The Pharisee's Banquet with Christ and Mary Magdalene
Canvas, 386 × 318 cm
Acquisition: 1815, from France in exchange for *The Wedding at Cana* by Paolo Veronese,(cat. 377)
Latest restoration: 1962

Nicola Renieri
(Nicolas Régnier, Maubeuge 1591-Venice 1667)

Allegorical Figure
Canvas, 140 × 68 cm
Acquisition: 1838, following the Napoleonic suppressions, (cat. 553)
Latest restoration: 1958

Joseph Heintz il Giovane
(Ausburg c. 1600-Venice 1678)

The Four Crowned Saints Refuse to Worship Idols

Canvas, 266 × 169 cm
Acquisition: 1982, by purchase, (cat. 1365)

Pietro Berrettini da Cortona
(Cortona 1596-Rome 1669)

Daniel in the Lions' Den

Canvas, 440 × 223 cm
Acquisition: 1829, following the Napoleonic suppressions, (cat. 754)
Latest restoration: 1955

Luca Giordano
(Naples 1634-1705)

The Deposition

Canvas, 440 × 243 cm
Acquisition: 1829, following the Napoleonic suppressions, (cat. 643)
Latest restoration: 1961-62

Giulio Carpioni
(Venice? 1613-Vicenza 1679)

The Triumph of Silenus

Canvas, 96 × 79 cm
Acquisition: 1910, donation of Giuseppe Rossi, (cat. 739)
Latest restoration: 1956

Sebastiano Mazzoni
(1611-1678)

The Mystical Marriage of Saint Catherine

Canvas, 154 × 449 cm
Acquisition: 1965, from Santa Caterina, (cat. 1331)
Latest restoration: 1956

Saint Catherine Disputing with the Philosophers

Canvas, 167 × 445 cm
Acquisition: 1965, from Santa Caterina, (cat. 1330)
Latest restoration: 1956

Giovanni Antonio Fumiani
(Venice 1650-1710)

Christ with the Doctors

Canvas, 553 × 314 cm
Acquisition: 1988, from the state depository, (cat. 1390)
Latest restoration: 1988-90

Gregorio Lazzarini
(Venice 1655 – Villabona 1730)

Circumcision

Canvas, 553 × 314 cm
Acquisition: 1988, from the state
depository (cat. 1391)
Latest restoration: 1988-90

Alessandro Magnasco
(Genoa c. 1667 – c. 1749)
Anton Francesco Peruzzini
(Ancona 1650/55 – Milan
1720/25)

*Landscape with Praying Monks,
or The Great Wood*

Canvas,174 × 237 cm
Acquisition 1989, upon
the exercise of a right
of pre-emption (cat. 1389)

Giambattista Piazzetta
(Venice 1683-1754)

Christ Crucifixed the Two Thieves

Canvas, 76 × 52 cm
Acquisition: 1905, by purchase
(cat. 719)
Latest restoration: 1995

Michele Marieschi
(Venice 1710-1743)

View with Bridge

Canvas 62 × 95 cm
Acquisition: 1908, by purchase
(cat. 715)

Francesco Zugno
(Venice 1709-1787)

Saint Benedict

Canvas, 57,5 × 45,5 cm
Acquisition: 1977, by purchase
(cat.1347)
Latest restoration: 1974-75

Saint Bruno

Canvas, 57,5 × 45,5 cm
Acquisition: 1977, by purchase
(cat. 1348)
Latest restoration: 1974-75

Giuseppe Bazzani
(Mantua 1690-1769)

Adoration of the Magi

Canvas 106 × 79 cm
Acquisition: 1909, donated
by A. Salvadori (cat. 747)
Latest restoration: 1938

Rest in Egypt

Canvas, l06 × 79 cm
Acquisition 1909, donated
by A. Salvadori (cat. 748)
Latest restoration: 1938

Francesco Hayez
(Venice 1791 – Milan 1882)

Destruction of the Temple of Jerusalem

Canvas, 183 × 82 cm
Acquisition 1868, by donation
from the artist (cat. 756)
Latest restoration: 1989

Giambattista Mariotti
(ascribed to)
(Venice 1694 – Padua c. 1765)

*Saint Ignatius of Loyola Before
the Pope*

Canvas, 119 × 160 cm
Acquisition: 1960, by purchase
(cat. 1321)
Latest restoration: 1960-61

Giandomenico Tiepolo
(Venice 1727-1804)

The Institution of the Eucharist

Canvas 137 × l00 cm
Acquisition 1807, from the
old Accademia (cat. 488)
Latest restoration: 1960

Alessandro Longhi
(Venice 1733-1813)

The Architect Tommaso Temanza

Canvas, 72 × 55 cm
Acquisition: 1845, donated
by Francesco Lazzati (cat. 478)
Latest restoration: 1994

Portrait of Doge Alvise Mocenigo

Canvas, 82 × 65 cm
Acquisition: 1807, from
the old Accademia (cat. 473)
Latest restoration: 1958

Portrait of Doge Paolo Renier

Canvas, 81 × 66 cm
Acquisition: 1807, from
the old Accademia (cat. 477)
Latest restoration: 1961

Madonna

Canvas, 44 × 36 cm
Acquisition: 1959, after Napoleonic
suppressions (cat. 1332)
Latest restoration: 1961

Luigi Crespi
(Bologna 1708-1779)

Self-Portrait

Canvas, 114 × 95 cm
Acquisition: 1807, from
the old Accademia (cat. 482)

Domenico Pellegrini
(Galliera Veneta 1759 – Rome
1840)

*Portrait of the Engraver Francesco
Bartolozzi*

Canvas, 106 × 89 cm
Acquisition: 1834, by donation
from the artist (cat. 453)
Latest restoration: 1958

Giovanni Migliara
(Alessandria 1785 – Milan 1837)

View of a Shoreside Church

Canvas, 47 × 56 cm
Acquisition: 1903, by purchase
(cat. 710)
Latest restoration: 1903

Select bibliography

S. Moschini Marconi,
*Gallerie dell'Accademia di Venezia.
Opere d'arte dei secoli XIV e XV*,
Rome 1955

Id., *Gallerie dell'Accademia di
Venezia. Opere d'arte del secolo XVI*,
Rome 1962

Id., *Gallerie dell'Accademia
di Venezia. Opere d'arte
dei secoli
XVII, XVIII, XIX*, Rome 1970

G. Nepi Scirè, *Gallerie
dell'Accademia di Venezia.
Storia della collezione dei Disegni*,
Milan 1982

G. Nepi Scirè, F. Valcanover,
Gallerie dell'Accademia di Venezia,
Milan 1985

Gallerie dell'Accademia. Acquisizioni,
edited by G. Nepi Scirè, Venice
1988

G. Nepi Scirè, *I capolavori dell'arte
veneziana. Le Gallerie dell'Accademia*,
Venice 1991

Id., *Le Gallerie dell'Accademia*,
Rome 1993

Id., *Le Gallerie dell'Accademia
di Venezia*, Venice 1994

Id., *Guida alla Quadreria*,
Venice 1995 (with bibliography)

and:

A.A.V.V., *Giovanni Gerolamo Savoldo*,
exhibition catalogue, Milan 1990

A.A.V.V., *Tiziano*, exhibition
catalogue edited by F. Valcanover,
Venice 1990

A.A.V.V., *La pittura nel Veneto.
Il Quattrocento*, 2 vols., Milan 1990

A.A.V.V., *Jacopo Bassano ca 1510-1592*,
exhibition catalogue edited by B.L.
Brown, P. Marini, Bologna 1992

A.A.V.V., *Piero e Urbino. Piero
e le corti rinascimentali*, exhibition
catalogue edited by P. Dal
Poggetto, Venice 1992

A.A.V.V., *Andrea Mantegna*,
exhibition catalogue edited
by S. Martineau, London 1992

A.A.V.V., *Leonardo & Venezia*,
exhibition catalogue, Milan 1992

A.A.V.V., *La pittura nel Veneto.
Il Trecento*, Milan 1992

A.A.V.V., *Le siècle de Titien*,
exhibition catalogue edited
by M. Laclotte, Paris 1993

A.A.V.V., *Pietro Longhi*, exhibition
catalogue edited by A. Mariuz,
G. Pavanello, G.D. Romanelli,
Milan 1993

A.A.V.V., *Bessarione e l'umanesimo*,
exhibition catalogue edited by
G. Fiaccadori, Naples 1994

A.A.V.V., *Jacopo Tintoretto. Ritratti*,
exhibition catalogue, edited by
P. Rossi, Milan 1994

A.A.V.V., *La pittura nel Veneto.
Il Settecento*, Milan 1995

A.A.V.V., *Bernardo Strozzi. Genova
1581/82–Venezia 1644*, exhibition
catalogue edited by E. Gavazza,
G. Nepi Scirè, G. Rotondi
Terminiello, Milan 1995

A.A.V.V., *Tiziano Amor Sacro e Amor
Profano*, exhibition catalogue, Milan
1995

A.A.V.V., *Splendori del Settecento
veneziano*, exhibition catalogue,
Milan 1995

A.A.V.V., *Il Trecento Riminese*, edited by D. Benati, Milan 1995

A.A.V.V., *Tiepolo*, exhibition catalogue edited by K. Christiansen, Milan 1996

A.A.V.V., "Il soffitto degli Scalzi di Giambattista Tiepolo", in *Quaderno della Soprintendenza per i Beni Artistici e Storici di Venezia*, 21, Venice 1997

A.A.V.V., *Lorenzo Lotto il genio inquieto del Rinascimento*, exhibition catalogue, Milan 1997

J. Anderson, *Giorgione peintre de la "brièveté poétique". Catalogue raisonné*, Paris 1996

A. Ballarin, *Jacopo Bassano. Scritti 1964-1995*, edited by V. Romani, 5 vols., Cittadella 1995

S. Campbell, *Cosmè Tura di Ferrara*, New Haven 1998

C.E. Cohen, *The Art of Giovanni Antonio da Pordenone*, Cambridge 1995

O. Ferrari, G. Scavizzi, *Luca Giordano. L'opera completa*, 2 vols., Naples 1992

P. Fortini Brown, *La pittura nell'età di Carpaccio. I grandi cicli narrativi*, Venice 1992

M. Gemin, F. Pedrocco, *Giambattista Tiepolo. Dipinti. Opera completa*, Verona 1993

A. Gentili, "Giovanni Bellini, la bottega, i quadri di devozione", in *Venezia Cinquecento*, I, 2, July-December 1991

R. Goffen, *Giovanni Bellini*, Milan 1990

B. Hope, "A new Documento about Titian's Pietà", in *Sight & Insight: Essay on Art and Culture in Honour of E.H. Gombrich at 85*, London 1994

Id., *Le Storie di Carpaccio. Venezia, i turchi, gli ebrei*, Venice 1996

P. Humfrey, *Carpaccio. Catalogo completo dei dipinti*, Florence 1991

Id., *The Altarpiece in Renaissance Venice*, New Haven-London 1993

Id., *I teleri della Sala dell'Albergo nella Scuola di San Marco*, Venice 1994

Id., *I teleri della Sala dell'Albergo nella Scuola di San Marco*, Venice 1994

Id., *Jacopo Amigoni*, Cremona 1994

Id., *Le Storie di Carpaccio. Venezia, i turchi, gli ebrei*, Venice 1996

Id., *Titian's Women*, New Haven-London 1997

G. Marin, "Vittore Belliniano e Lorenzo Lotto", in *Studi di storia dell'Arte*, 576, Todi 1995

S. Mason, *Carpaccio. I grandi cicli pittorici*, Milan 2000

G. Nepi Scirè, "Venezia e la pittura intorno al 1500", in *Leonardo & Venezia*, Milan 1992

Id, *Carpaccio. Storie di Sant'Orsola*, Milan 2000

T. Pignatti, F. Pedrocco, *Veronese. Catalogo completo*, 2 vols., Milan 1995

A.B. Rave, *Gaspare Traversi Heiterkeit im Schatten*, exhibition catalogue, Stuttgart 2003

P. Rossi, *Francesco Maffei*, Milan 1991

E.A. Safarik, *Fetti*, Milan 1990

A. Scarpa Sonino, *Marco Ricci*, Milan 1991

V. Sgarbi, *Carpaccio*, Milan 1994

D. Thiebaut, "Le Christ à la colonne d'Antonello de Messina", *Les Dossier des Musée du Louvre*, Paris 1993

Bellini a Vicenza, edited by F. Rigon, E.M. Dal Pozzolo, exhibition catalogue, Vicenza 2003

Carlo Crivelli alle Gallerie dell'Accademia. Un capolavoro ricomposto, exhibition catalogue, Milan 2002

Carpaccio pittore di storie, edited by G. Nepi Scirè, exhibition catalogue, Venice 2004

"Cristoforo Orsetti e i suoi quadri di 'perfetta mano'", in *Figure di collezionisti a Venezia tra Cinque e Seicento*, edited by L. Borean, S. Mason, Udine 2002

Fra Galgario. Le seduzioni del ritratto del '700 europeo, edited by F. Rossi, exhibition catalogue, Milan 2003

Giorgione. "Le maraviglie dell'arte", edited by G. Nepi Scirè, S. Rossi, exhibition catalogue, Venice 2003

Il colore ritrovato. Bellini a Venezia, edited by R. Goffen, G. Nepi Scirè, exhibition catalogue, Milan 2000

Il Gran teatro del Mondo. L'anima e il volto del Settecento, edited by F. Caroli, exhibition catalogue, Milan 2003

Il Rinascimento a Venezia e la pittura del Nord ai tempi di Bellini, Dürer, Tiziano, edited by B. Aikema, B.L. Brown, G. Nepi Scirè, exhibition catalogue, Milan 2000

Il Trecento adriatico. Paolo Veneziano e la pittura tra Oriente ed Occidente, edited by F. Flores d'Arcais, G. Gentili, exhibition catalogue, Cinisello Balsamo 2002

Le ceneri violette di Giorgione. Natura e maniera tra Tiziano e Caravaggio, edited by V. Sgarbi, exhibition catalogue, Milan 2004

Tiepolo, la Crocifissione di Burano. Un capolavoro restaurato, edited by G. Manieri Elia, A. Mariuz, G. Nepi Scirè, exhibition catalogue, Venice 2003

Titian, edited by D. Jaffé, exhibition catalogue, London 2003